Research in Criminology

Series Editors
Alfred Blumstein
David P. Farrington

Research in Criminology

continued after index

Rudy Haapanen

Selective Incapacitation and the Serious Offender

A Longitudinal Study of
Criminal Career Patterns

With 11 Illustrations

Springer-Verlag
New York Berlin Heidelberg
London Paris Tokyo Hong Kong

Rudy Haapanen
Research Division, California Youth Authority, Sacramento, California 95823, USA

Series Editors

Alfred Blumstein
School of Urban and Public Affairs, Carnegie-Mellon University, Pittsburgh, Pennsylvania 15213, USA

David P. Farrington
Institute of Criminology, University of Cambridge, CB3 9DT, England

Library of Congress Cataloging-in-Publication Data
Haapanen, Rudy A.
   Selective incapacitation and the serious offender: a longitudinal
study of criminal career patterns/Rudy A. Haapanen.
     p. cm.—(Research in criminology)
   Bibliography: p.
   Includes index.
   ISBN 0-387-97051-7
   1. Criminal behavior—California—Longitudinal studies.
2. Recidivism—California—Longitudinal studies. 3. Imprisonment—
California—Longitudinal studies. I. Title. II. Series.
HV6793.C2H33   1989
364.3'09794—dc20   89-11434

Printed on acid-free paper.

Typeset by Thomson Press, New Delhi, India.
Printed and bound by Edwards Brothers, Inc., Ann Arbor, Michigan.
Printed in the United States of America.

9 8 7 6 5 4 3 2 1

ISBN 0-387- 97051-7 Springer-Verlag New York Berlin Heidelberg
ISBN 3-540- 97051-7 Springer-Verlag Berlin Heidelberg New York

Foreword

And if thy right hand offend thee, cut it off, and cast it from thee; for it is profitable for thee that one of thy members should perish, and not that thy whole body should be cast into hell.

Matthew 5.30

The great War on Poverty of the 1960s focused on the root causes of crime, unemployment, lack of education, and discrimination. It was eventually agreed that the War on Poverty failed as a crime control program, and the focus of policy shifted toward more proximate causes of crime. In fact, it seems safe to say that since the 1960s, the United States has looked primarily to the criminal justice system to solve its crime problem.

With the 1990s upon us, what can we say about the success of crime control policies that rely on the criminal justice system? The picture, taken one approach or program at a time, is not good. It is now generally agreed that the criminal justice system fails to rehabilitate offenders, to make them less likely to commit criminal acts as a result of treatment or training; that the system fails to deter potential offenders, to make them less likely to commit criminal acts out of fear of penal sanctions; and that such programs as increased police patrols, reinstatement of the death penalty, and modification of the exclusionary rule are unlikely to have much effect on crime, at least within the limits imposed on them by reasonable assessments of their costs.

The record suggests that criminal justice solutions to crime have been no more effective than root-cause solutions. How then can we explain the continuing enthusiasm for criminal justice system solutions and the apparent lack of interest in alternative remedies to crime? The answer seems to lie in the promise of a criminal justice program as direct and simple as cutting off the hand of the thief, a program that makes crime impossible by locking up criminals. This program, selective incapacitation, is the subject of Rudy Haapanen's book.

The significance of a book dealing with the last hope of those who would use the police power of the state to control crime is hard to overestimate. If selective incapacitation turns out to have the potential envisioned, we will have at last a cheap and easy device for reducing crime. If, however, selective incapacitation is unable to deliver reductions in crime consistent with its costs, it will be difficult for the criminal justice system to continue to demand, with a straight face, an ever-larger share of tax dollars. If selective incapacitation is unable to deliver the reductions promised, it will be difficult to avoid fundamental rethinking of the crime problem and what we might do about it.

So, we have here a study whose question has implications far beyond the success or failure of a single program, a study that bears directly on the soundness of a general policy, on the adequacy of an entire way of thinking about crime. Dr. Haapanen's study is, in my view, more than adequate to the task, and should be treated accordingly.

A successful program of selective incapacitation depends on the ability of the criminal justice system to identify a relatively small group of offenders likely to commit serious crimes at a high rate over an extended period of time. A politically feasible program of selective incapacitation would base such identification on legally relevant information routinely available to the criminal justice system. This longitudinal study of a large number of high-rate offenders in California provides direct answers to the major questions facing such a program: Do the required serious and persistent offenders exist? Can they be identified early in their careers? What effect would incapacitating them for longer periods have on the crime rate? Are members of some racial groups more likely than others to meet the requirements of such a program?

The answers to these questions provided by Dr. Haapanen are clear and, to my mind, convincing. He tells us that for a variety of reasons incapacitation, selective or otherwise, is not the long-awaited answer to the crime problem. Unfortunately, it is hard to hear the message of careful and reasonable research over the din of prison construction and the clamor for more of it. As a result, it will undoubtedly be awhile before the wisdom of Dr. Haapanen's findings prevails. In the meantime, people who read his book can console themselves with the knowledge that work has already been done on the foundation of an enlightened crime control policy.

Travis Hirschi

Acknowledgments

Many people have contributed greatly to the research and to the making of this book. To each, I owe a sincere debt of gratitude. To some, I owe special thanks.

The research was conducted under a grant from the Offender Classification and Prediction of Criminal Behavior program at the National Institute of Justice, U.S. Department of Justice (Grant#83-IJ-CX-0034). Additional resources were provided by the California Youth Authority. At all times, I was encouraged to use my own professional judgement in conducting the research and reporting the findings. Therefore, the findings, conclusions, and opinions contained in this book do not necessarily represent the official position or policy of the U.S. Department of Justice, the National Institute of Justice, the California Youth Authority, or the State of California. I would like to thank Richard Laymon and Richard Linster, both of NIJ, for their continued support and encouragement during the project. Their efforts contribute greatly to the enhancement of criminological research in this country.

My greatest debt is to Carl Jesness, who not only guided me through my growth as a researcher in this area, but who provided the impetus and the data for embarking on the longitudinal study of former California Youth Authority wards. He undertook the original studies that gathered data on these young offenders and received funding for the first of our follow-up studies. I am very grateful for his tutelage and his fellowship through the years.

Core members of the research team included Beverly Lozano, co-investigator, Cathi Heffington, clerical support, and two outstanding graduate students from the California State University at Sacramento: Ron Gottfredson and Kathy Houston-Hencken. Their assistance with data collection, coding, and analysis was invaluable. They also freely contributed their knowledge, insights, advice, and good humor to the project throughout.

Other project staff included Janet Smith, Diane Reardon, Katie White, Patricia Hoover, Petra Edwards, Petronia Collins, Lori McGregor, Janice Anderson, and Tony Landrum, all graduate students at California State University, Sacramento. Their individual contributions are gratefully acknowledged.

Staff of the California Department of Corrections and County Probation Departments were extremely helpful in providing lists of potential sample members and in making the case file data available for coding. Dave Park, the keeper of the file room at the Correctional Medical Facility at Vacaville, put up with weeks of having three or four project staffers pull files and code data. Similarly, probation staff throughout the state provided access to their case files. On request, many even pulled files themselves and mailed the data to us, saving a tremendous amount of time and effort. Without this help, we could never have gathered the data on social lifestyle and incarceration variables.

Thanks are also due to friends, colleagues, and administrators at the California Youth Authority. The encouragement of the CYA administration for pursuing basic research in criminology is noteworthy and greatly appreciated. Jean Bottcher, Norm Skonovd, and Ted Palmer, colleagues in the Research Division, made the research better in many ways through their personal interest and probing questions. Special thanks are extended to Craig Brown, Undersecretary, and Sue Loustalot, Deputy Secretary, of the Youth and Adult Correctional Agency, for meticulously reading every word of the manuscript and for providing their insights into the policy implications of the findings.

I am grateful to Travis Hirschi, who first sparked my interest in the study of crime and delinquency when I served as his teaching assistant at the University of California at Davis, for his willingness to contribute a Foreword to this book. His down-to-earth approach to understanding crime, along with his commitment to scholarship, has inspired me over the years and has served as a model for my own research.

Finally, I would like to thank my wife, Lori, for her support through the late nights at work and the hours of restlessness that seem to inevitably accompany such endeavors.

The support, help, and approval of all of these individuals made this project possible, but they do not necessarily imply agreement with the interpretations or conclusions. Any errors, omissions, or misinterpretations are solely my responsibility.

Biographical Sketch

Rudy Haapanen is a Research Specialist in the Research Division of the California Youth Authority (CYA). He received his Ph.D. in Sociology from the University of California at Davis in 1976. Since joining the CYA, Dr. Haapanen has undertaken several major, federally funded studies, including a statewide evaluation of delinquency prevention projects in California; an exploration of advanced analytic methods for use in evaluative research; a long-term follow-up study exploring the usefulness of early psychological, attitudinal, and demographic information for predicting adult criminality among former CYA wards; and two longitudinal studies of adult criminal career patterns of serious youthful offenders. His publications include *Youth Service Bureaus: An Evaluation of Nine California Youth Service Bureaus* (with David Rudisill), *Early Identification of the Chronic Offender* (with Carl Jesness), and *Alternatives to Analysis of Covariance for Estimating Treatment Effects in Criminal Justice Evaluation: Comparative Results*. In addition to continuing his research on criminal careers, he is currently in charge of research involving parole services and is helping to develop a prediction-oriented classification system for the California Youth Authority.

Contents

List of Tables

List of Figures

Chapter 1
Introduction

Every year countless millions of dollars are spent trying to combat crime. New programs, new approaches, and new policies are continuously being tried and discarded in favor of still newer ones. In this process, empirically derived knowledge often takes a back seat to public sentiment. The public wants to feel safer, more secure, more *powerful* in the face of what appears to be a growing menace. The current "get tough on crime" approach is, in part, a way of striking back. Still, public policy cannot ignore the facts. The public wants policies that *work*—not policies that feel good. Unfortunately, crime is a complex phenomenon, and solid information about important issues is often lacking. In the absence of good information, beliefs—assumptions, if you will—about crime and its perpetrators must suffice. Researchers engaged in the pursuit of a better understanding of crime seek in one way or another to fill the gaps in our knowledge and thereby bring knowledge and belief into closer harmony. A solid foundation of knowledge, in turn, may set the stage for greater rationality in criminal justice policy.

One major gap in our knowledge about crime is in the area of changes that occur in criminal behavior as offenders move through life. Most studies of offenders focus on prisoners (who constitute an easily accessible population) and study their behavior for only a short span of time—usually the periods immediately before and after imprisonment. But what about offenders who never go to prison? What about other time periods in these offenders' lives? Why do some offenders go to prison early in life, while others enter later? Is it merely luck, or has their behavior changed? Does criminal behavior decline as offenders age or do offenders simply stop altogether at some point? Is the amount of criminal behavior committed by offenders related to their employment or family life or use of drugs, as these change over time?

The present study attempts to answer these questions by investigating the patterns of criminal behavior that occurred over 10 to 15 years for some 1300 men whose early criminal involvement was serious enough to result in commitment to California Youth Authority (state-level) institutions. This sample provided a unique opportunity for studying the ebb and flow of criminality over the years of greatest adult criminal involvement. The main focus of the study was on changes in criminal behavior as these men moved through their twenties and into their thirties. Some of them served prison terms; others did not. Some committed many crimes during these years, while others committed only a few. Patterns of criminality could therefore be studied over different levels of criminal involvement. In some analyses, the sample was expanded to include offenders who were not so seriously involved in criminal behavior at a young age; these analyses focused on differences in overall seriousness of criminality and on some of the factors associated with these differences. Information from prison and probation files was used to explore the relationship of employment, family status, and drug use to changes in criminal behavior over the young adult years.

So why is the understanding of *these* patterns important? Besides having intrinsic value as basic information about criminal behavior, these patterns have profound implications for what can be done about crime. A better understanding of such patterns provides a firmer basis for evaluating both current policies and those that are offered as potential improvements.

Indeed, the primary impetus for the present study was to better understand the potential benefits of one of the more popular, and controversial, policy notions in the area of crime reduction: *selective incapacitation*. This idea starts with the premise that prison serves primarily as a means for keeping offenders off the streets and therefore unable to prey on others. The main function of prison, in this view, is (or should be) to *incapacitate offenders*. Prison space, however, is both expensive and increasingly scarce, and the use of increased prison sentences to reduce crime (relative to current levels) may not be very practical from a policy standpoint. The answer, some would argue, lies in being *selective* in imposing the longer sentences. Recent research indicates that offenders differ greatly in the rate at which they commit crimes; most offenders commit only a few crimes per year, while a small minority of offenders not only commit crimes at very high rates but appear to be responsible for the majority of crimes (Chaiken and Chaiken, 1982). If the payoff is too low (and the cost too high) for keeping *all* offenders in prison longer, why not increase sentences only for the high-rate offenders? By *selectively incapacitating* these high-rate offenders, the argument goes, it may be possible to significantly increase the crime-reduction payoff associated with given levels of prison use.

Additional research evidence suggests that high rates of criminal behavior appear to be associated with certain characteristics of an offender's past behavior and present circumstances (Greenwood, 1982). These findings point to the possibility that the high-rate offenders could be identified on the basis of characteristics that many would argue *should* be used to set sentence lengths (number of prior convictions, for example). Selective incapacitation seems to provide the best of both worlds: as a policy, it allows society to get "tough" on the worst offenders in the name of pursuing a rational strategy aimed at fighting crime.

At first glance, it may not be obvious that such an argument rests on certain fundamental assumptions concerning *patterns* of criminal behavior. The problem, after all, would seem to be a simple matter of predicting which offenders would be most likely to commit crimes at high rates once released from prison. These offenders could then be required to serve an additional year or so behind bars. Their behavior at other times would not be of interest, except as a basis for predicting their post-prison criminality. Arguments for selective incapacitation, however, tend to go one step further, assuming that high-rate offenders constitute a *stable subset* of the larger population of criminal offenders. Such an assumption suggests the possibility that selective incapacitation could have a substantial effect on crime in the larger society. High-volume offenders, who are the primary targets of the policy, are assumed to contribute their disproportionate share of crimes by maintaining a relatively high rate of criminal activity throughout their active adult criminal lives (their "criminal careers"). The more effective the policy is at identifying and incapacitating these high-rate offenders, the fewer of them there would be on the street and the lower the overall crime rate would be. Only if criminal behavior among serious offenders is *stable* can there be a stable cadre of high-rate criminals; stability, therefore, is critical to the concept of selective incapacitation. To date, however, there is no strong, direct evidence for this kind of stability.

In addition to a host of moral, legal, and ethical issues surrounding the adoption of such a policy, there are other assumptions underlying the concept of selective incapacitation that raise serious questions about its ultimate value. Similarly, there are a number of good reasons besides incapacitation for sentencing serious offenders to prison. None of these issues, however, was of major concern to the present study. Rather, the focus was on trying to determine whether a policy of selectively sentencing offenders to prison for longer terms *could work* to substantially reduce crime.

To that end, the study was organized primarily around investigating, to the extent possible using official data, whether the criminal behavior of the offenders in this sample was reasonably stable. Stability was analyzed directly, in terms of comparisons over time, using methods that minimize the problems associated with using official data. Stability was also assessed indirectly, through focusing on certain corollary assumptions, all of which flow from the logical necessity that for criminal behavior to be stable over an offender's entire career, it must be largely unaffected by social or environmental (i.e., situational) influences. Specifically, the policy assumes that criminal behavior will be unrelated to such factors as age or race (since these can be seen as indicators of social or environmental differences) and will be unaffected by jail, prison, or other correctional interventions. The relationships between these factors and criminal behavior were analyzed to help establish the reasonableness of the "stability" assumption.

In the pages that follow, the concept of selective incapacitation and the assumptions upon which it rests will be described in somewhat more detail. A general overview of the present study and the organization of this book will follow that discussion.

The Concept of Selective Incapacitation

Interest in the feasibility of policies of selectively incapacitating particular offenders was spurred by research indicating that small minority of offenders was responsible for the majority of crimes, whether measured in terms of police contacts among the general population (Wolfgang, Figlio, and Sellin, 1972) or in terms of self-reported crimes among prison inmates (Peterson and Braiker, 1980; Chaiken and Chaiken, 1982). By focusing scarce prison resources on this high-rate minority, the reasoning goes, the greatest return on society's crime-fighting investment could be realized. In fact, proponents of selective incapacitation have suggested that a well-designed policy could reduce the amount of crime in society as a whole by a significant amount. Greenwood (1982), for example, argued that a selective sentencing policy aimed at adult robbers could reduce the number of armed robberies by as much as 20%, while keeping the number of incarcerated armed robbers at current levels. Given the ever-present public concern over rising costs related to fighting crime, the concept of selective incapacitation has a certain seductive appeal, and research suggesting that such policies are both practical and economical has generated a great deal of interest in criminal justice circles (Blumstein, Cohen, Roth, and Visher, 1986; Cohen, 1983).

While simple common sense would suggest that more is to be gained from locking up high-rate offenders than low-rate offenders, the extent of that gain is not easily or unambiguously determined. The different techniques that have been employed in this regard have been carefully reviewed by Cohen (1978, 1983). Of interest here are the most recent methods employed in this line of research: the use of "models" of crime and the criminal justice system. Such models were used by Greenwood (1982) in his controversial study and have been used in subsequent research in this area as well (Cohen, 1983, 1986). These studies have built upon a sizable body of research that has attempted to understand the effects of changing certain aspects of the criminal justice system—in this case, the length of incarceration for various offenders. This body of research began with the work of Avi-Itzhak and Shinnar (1973), who developed mathematical models of crime and the criminal justice system response. These models specify the general relationships among criminal behavior; the probabilities of arrest, conviction, and incarceration; and the length of incarceration. Correctly specified, such models could, first, establish a steady-state description of crime and criminal justice, including the proportion of active offenders who are incarcerated at any one time and the amount of crime that is prevented through that incarceration (i.e., the incapacitative effect of current incarceration policies). Next, by altering various parameters of the model, estimates of the effects of various changes in criminal justice policies could be derived.[1] For example, estimates of the trade-off between reductions in crime and increases in prison populations resulting from particular sentencing policies could be estimated (Blumstein, Cohen, and Nagin, 1978).

Early work with these models used single estimates of offense rates as well as single estimates of the various other parameters of the model (e.g., the probability of arrest for any particular crime). They were subsequently modified by Greenwood (1982) to include separate estimates of offense rates for low-, medium-, and high-rate offenders and different probabilities of going to prison, if convicted, for these three types of offenders. With these parameter estimates, the model was used to estimate the incapacitative effects of policies that included different lengths of incarceration for these groups. Greenwood concluded from his study that a significant amount of crime reduction could be derived from policies that kept the high-rate offenders in prison longer and released the low-rate offenders early. These "selective incapacitation" policies could thereby achieve this crime-deduction benefit with no increase in prison use. Recent research using similar models on the same data produced similar, though reduced, estimates of the potential effects of these policies (Visher, 1986).

Assumptions Underlying the Concept and Models

Before discussing the assumption of offense-rate stability, which is most relevant to *selective* incapacitation, two assumptions that are critical to the notion that incapacitation can have *any* effect on the level of crime in society must first be acknowledged. For incarceration to have an effect, two critical conditions must be met: (1) that the incapacitated offenders would, in fact, commit crimes during the period of incapacitation were they free to do so, and (2) that the crimes prevented by incapacitating these offenders would not be committed by others instead.

The first condition is not difficult to meet, especially at the aggregate level. No type of intervention (short of the death penalty) has produced a recidivism rate of zero. Therefore, by locking offenders up for an additional year, it is fairly certain that *some* of the offenders would be prevented from committing *some* number of crimes. It is not so likely, however, that *every* identified offender would continue to commit crimes during that period—some retiring from crime altogether and others simply delaying their return to crime. Incapacitating these offenders would produce no crime-reduction benefit. Particular policies, therefore, are often judged in terms of the expected number of nonoffenders that they would subject to increased incarceration, both

---

[1] Since the focus of the present study was not on the details of the models, but on their underlying assumptions, such details will not be described fully here. These models, as well as other research that has attempted to estimate incapacitation effects, are described in detail (and critically reviewed) by Jacqueline Cohen (1983).

because of the legal/ethical problems involved (Blackmore and Welsh, 1983; von Hirsch and Gottfredson, 1983–84; Cohen, 1983) and because the incarceration of these offenders reduces the overall benefits of these policies.

The second condition—that other offenders will not commit the crimes that otherwise would have been committed by the incapacitated offender—is not so easy to assume. Included here are the conditions that no new offenders would be recruited into crime to take the incapacitated offenders' place and that the offender is not a member of groups that would continue to commit crimes at the same rate in his absence. It is reasonable to assume that at least some crimes would be affected by "market" conditions (drug sales, for example) and that the removal of one offender could easily result in his being replaced, but there has been little research on this issue, primarily because it deals with the basic nature and etiology of crime in society. (It could not, for example, be investigated using populations of known offenders.) Research on incapacitation has therefore tended to focus primarily on predatory crimes (assault, robbery, burglary), which are considered somewhat more likely to be single-offender crimes. Nevertheless, the issue is still recognized by supporters and critics alike as an important, and unresolved, one. Those attempting to investigate the merits of selective incapacitation policies therefore generally allude to its importance and then proceed to ignore it, treating it as an assumption upon which their research on the "potential effects" of incapacitation rests. The same will be done here; the present research focused, instead, on those issues that could be addressed with the present data.

The Assumption of Stability

The assumption that individual rates of criminal behavior are reasonably stable is not critical to the notion of *incapacitation*, but plays a fundamental role both in arguments for *selective* incapacitation and in the models currently used to estimate the potential effects of such a policy. In fact, the assumption arose in the context of developing these models, but has gained some wider acceptance as a way of characterizing criminal careers. That acceptance, in turn, has served to support the idea that there is a group of high-rate offenders out there whose incarceration could produce a significant reduction in overall crime.

Early research using these models (Shinnar and Shinnar, 1975) was hampered by a lack of information on the rate of individual criminal activity (commonly termed "lambda") and the conditional probabilities of arrest, conviction, and incarceration. The problem was handled through the use of rather arbitrary estimates of offense rates and by two major simplifying assumptions: (1) that all offenders commit crimes at the same overall rate throughout their active careers, and (2) that the probabilities of arrest, conviction, and incarceration are equal for all criminal acts (and all offenders) and independent of one another. Corollaries of the first of these assumptions are that offense rates are unaffected by incarceration (no rehabilitative or criminogenic effects of prison) and that incapacitating some offenders does not affect the rates of criminal behavior among *other* offenders (no deterrent effects, for example). Under these assumptions, it was possible to estimate the rates and probabilities from data on reported crimes, arrests, convictions, and so on; these data are available from state and federal sources.

Theoretically, these assumptions could be relaxed to allow for different rates of criminal behavior among offenders and for different conditional probabilities of arrest, conviction, or incarceration. In fact, such a relaxation of these assumptions is necessary for the model to be used to estimate the effects of selective incapacitation policies. Similarly, it is theoretically possible that various systematic changes in rates of criminal behavior (such as declines by age—"maturation effects") could also be incorporated into the model, although the model would soon become very complex. It would not be possible, however, to allow for these rates to go up and down unsystematically, so that different individuals would be high-rate offenders at different times. Under these conditions, changes in sentence lengths could not be assumed to have specifiable preventive effects on particular offenders, since their individual crime rates could change during the interim.

Underlying these assumptions is an even more basic assumption that the amount of crime in society is a simple function of a "fixed" number of criminals committing crimes at a constant rate (which may differ across offenders) over their entire periods of active involvement in crime—their criminal careers.[2] Incapacitation serves to put some portion of those offenders out of circulation. Since the crimes they would have committed are assumed *not* to be committed by those offenders who remain on the street or by "new" recruits to the ranks of criminals, this incapacitation reduces the number of crimes accordingly. If all offenders committed crimes at the same rate, the incapacitative effect of any particular policy could be estimated simply by determining the proportion of offenders incarcerated under that policy. In research on the effects of selective incapacitation policies, rates of criminal behavior are allowed to differ, and the incapacitative effects are estimated as a function of the number of offenders incarcerated and their respective rates of criminal behavior (which are, again, assumed not to change over time). Greenwood (1982), for example, divided offenders into those with low, medium, and high self-reported offense rates, with average values of those rates used in the calculations.

Together, these assumptions suggest a conception of criminal careers as stable patterns of criminal behavior, differing among offenders in terms of intensity and length but not differing appreciably over time (except for relatively brief interludes of incapacitative incarceration). This conception, which serves mainly to describe the kind of criminal history implied by the above assumptions, has gained some acceptance among criminologists as a valid description of criminal careers (see Blumstein, Cohen, Roth, and Visher, 1986). In fact, a current research priority at the federal level is to learn more

---

[2] Specifically, criminal behavior is assumed to be randomly distributed throughout the career, as are arrests, convictions, and incarcerations (a "stochastic" model).

about criminal careers—their onset, duration, and their variations—and to identify methods of dealing with those offenders with the most active criminal careers—the "career criminals."[3] These particularly dangerous offenders, who can be counted on to be stably dangerous in the future, are regarded as a high-priority target for criminal justice research and policy.

Technically, of course, the concept of selective incapacitation does not require that offense rates be perfectly stable, as long as high-rate offenders can be identified for that period during which they would be incapacitated. However, the popular conception of selective incapacitation is that it is not simply directed at offenders who would have higher rates of criminal behavior, but at a select group of "high-rate offenders," in the "career criminals" sense. It is thus closely linked to the currently popular conception of criminal careers, which, by their nature, can be incorporated into the kinds of models described above.

While not directed specifically at the merits of selective incapacitation, some researchers have argued for the reasonableness of the stability assumption. Some recent research, they argue, appears to indicate that while *participation* in crime is strongly related to such social factors as race and age, offense *rates* among *active offenders* do not differ much (if at all) by race or age (Blumstein and Cohen, 1979). While these findings have been criticized on methodological grounds (Gottfredson and Hirschi, 1986), they have been widely cited as evidence that criminal behavior is relatively stable (Cohen, 1983; Farrington, 1986; Blumstein et al., 1986). Social factors such as ethnicity or age are argued to affect individuals primarily in terms of whether and when they embark on criminal careers and when they end those careers—behavior in the interim is apparently more-or-less immune to these social influences. Implicit in this view is the notion that criminal propensity is somehow part of the individual and that it is generally unaffected to any great extent by situational factors. While these arguments are generally used to justify using the modeling techniques in criminology, they also serve to support the concept of criminal careers, as stable patterns of criminal behavior. These arguments therefore also support the reasonableness, in principle, of selective incapacitation.

In addition to allowing for the estimation of incapacitative effects using models, stability in criminal behavior suggests the possibility that selective sentencing policies may be practical and straightforward to carry out. If criminal behavior patterns are manifestations of stable individual differences in criminal propensity, it seems reasonable that some clear indicators of that propensity could be identified sooner or later. Moreover, the earlier in life these high-rate offenders could be identified, the greater the potential crime

---

[3] Certain criminologists have viewed this development with considerable dismay. Because it stands on tenuous, untested, and (in their view) mistaken assumptions, the federal research emphasis on criminal careers (as conceptualized) is considered ill advised (Gottfredson and Hirschi, 1986).

reduction (longer sentences for each conviction).[4] If, in contrast, offense rates are unstable, predictions based on individual characteristics could not be expected to very accurately identify offenders who would have the highest rates of criminal behavior. To the extent that the offense rate is not determined by individual characteristics, it must be determined by "outside" (social, environmental, situational) characteristics, which are difficult to include in prediction equations.

Thus, current thinking about criminal careers and selective incapacitation presupposes a certain fundamental characteristic of criminal careers—a stable offense rate that is basically an outgrowth of individual criminal propensities. This feature serves both to make possible the estimation of selective incapacitation effects using models and to suggest the benefit and the practical feasibility of selective sentencing policies. Actual data to support this assumption of stability are, however, scarce and open to question (Gottfredson and Hirschi, 1986). Clearly, there is a need for solid information on patterns of criminal behavior over time, with an emphasis on how stable these patterns tend to be. Not only would such information be of intrinsic interest, it would help inform theories and research into practical policies.

The Present Study

The study on which this book is based involved, primarily, the investigation of patterns of adult criminal behavior over time among serious offenders. These offenders were either former California Youth Authority wards (released from institutions between 1960 and 1970), or adult prisoners or probationers who had convictions for robbery or burglary but who had no history of state-level juvenile commitments. Thus, they were all serious offenders at one time or another, and most were relatively serious offenders for some portion of their adult criminal careers. Arrest histories (all charged offenses), as well as background information and social history data obtained from prison and probation files, were coded for up to 20 years (age 18 to age 37), allowing for longitudinal analysis of patterns.

Of interest were a number of issues, the most important of which was the

---

[4]Some critics of recent research have pointed out, for example, that Greenwood's (1982) scale for identifying high-rate offenders was developed using retrospective data and was not validated in terms of its ability to identify high-rate offenders in the future (Blackmore and Welsh, 1983; Chaiken and Chaiken, 1984; Clear and Barry, 1983; Blumstein et al., 1986). Greenwood himself even agrees that the prediction scale should be validated prospectively. However, if offense rates are stable, individuals identified as high-rate offenders at any point in time could be expected to commit crimes at high rates at other times as well; consequently, they need only be identified once. Under these conditions, retrospective data would be just as valid for identifying high-rate offenders as prospective data.

degree of stability in criminal behavior. Issues such as differences in patterns of criminal behavior by race and age were explored to assess the applicability of earlier findings to the current sample and to ascertain the reasonableness of the contention that offense rates are unrelated to these important social factors. The report is organized around these issues, proceeding roughly from the simpler to the more complex. This organization allows the reader to first gain familiarity with the data and with some of the more clear-cut issues in the area of criminal career research.

Chapter 2 provides an overview of the study design: the nature of the samples, the types of data obtained, and the manner in which the data were coded and used to establish career indices. This nontechnical discussion is intended to provide enough information for readers to draw their own conclusions concerning the adequacy of the samples and findings upon which various conclusions were based.

Chapters 3 and 4 focus on the issues of the extent of participation in crime (for the sample as a whole and by race and age) and of average rates of arrest (again by race and age). The longitudinal data on former California Youth Authority wards permitted an examination not only of simple indices of involvement in crime but also of "career" characteristics, such as breadth of involvement and the extent of repetition for particular crime types. Thus, these chapters provide a detailed look at differences by race and age for offenders who began serious criminal careers early in life.

In Chapter 5, important methodological issues related to the use of individual-level data on rates of arrest are addressed. This chapter is devoted to understanding the limitations of the present data and establishing what might be expected, in terms of the observed stability of *arrest* rates, given reasonably stable rates of criminal *behavior*. Analyses were performed to establish both the reliabilities of the measures and "standards" against which to evaluate estimates of career stability over time.

Chapters 6 and 7 focus specifically on stability and change in offense behavior over time. Using the findings from Chapter 5 as a baseline, analyses focused on whether offense rates were more or less stable than might be expected, given the limitations imposed by the use of arrest-rate measures. In Chapter 6, somewhat arbitrary four-year blocks of ages are used to determine whether criminal behavior for these offenders was stable from one period to the next. In Chapter 7, similar analyses were performed for the four-year periods immediately before and after a major conviction—prison or probation sentence.

Chapter 8 presents the results of analyses aimed at determining the extent to which background and family characteristics, drug use, marital status, and employment were related to arrest rates over time. Separate analyses focused on characteristics related to postprison rates of criminality for those offenders who served adult prison terms.

Chapter 9 is devoted to the findings concerning potential incapacitative effects of lengthened terms for these offenders. These estimates, which were made directly from data on post-prison arrests, did not depend on assumptions of stability. As indications of possible effects of these policies on crime in society, however, they would still rest on an assumption that any prevented crimes would not have been committed by other offenders.

Finally, in Chapter 10, a summary of these findings is provided, and some of their implications for criminal justice research and policy are highlighted. Unfortunately, the nature of the findings make suggestions for positive programmatic proposals difficult. The study's main contributions are to general knowledge about criminal behavior patterns and the factors that seem to influence them. It is hoped that the reader will come away with a greater appreciation of the complexities of criminal behavior and a sense of caution concerning the currently popular, but simplistic, conception of criminal careers. It is also hoped that this study will further inform the debate as to the merits of selective incapacitation policies, which would appear to hold little promise as practical solutions to the problem of crime in our society.

Chapter 2
Sample and Methods

This research study began in 1961, when Dr. Carl Jesness decided to retain the data he had been collecting on young wards being treated at the Fricot Ranch, a camp maintained by the California Youth Authority (Jesness, 1965). He reasoned that these data might be useful in future years for long-term follow-up of these young delinquents. For similar reasons, he also retained the data collected during the Preston Typology Development Project (Jesness, 1969, 1971a) and The Youth Center Research Project (Jesness, 1971b, 1975; Jesness, DeRisi, McCormick, and Wedge, 1972). In all, over 2800 wards were involved in these three research projects. In 1978, the decision was made to study the subsequent criminal histories of these wards. The purpose was twofold: to determine the long-term expectations for California Youth Authority wards and to assess the extent to which the information collected during the three research projects could aid in identifying those with the most active and/or dangerous adult criminal behavior patterns.

That follow-up study (Haapanen and Jesness, 1982) analyzed data on subsequent arrests (using the most serious charge for each arrest incident) over a 10 to 15 year period. In addition, attitudinal, background, and psychological data retained from the earlier studies were used in an attempt to predict subsequent offense behavior. Juvenile and young adult offenders are committed to the California Youth Authority because of serious and/or extensive involvement in criminality at an early age. For example, most of these juvenile offenders had more than three prior police contacts—the number that Wolfgang, Figlio, and Sellin (1972) found to be indicative of chronic criminality. It was felt that such a sample would contain enough relatively active offenders to reduce the research problems ordinarily associated with the low population base-rate for chronic criminal behavior. In fact, the reverse was found: only 6% of the simple remained arrest-free during the follow-up period, 80% were arrested for some kind of felony offense, and 66% showed an arrest for a violent crime. These figures contrast sharply with estimates of criminal involvement in the general population: 50 to 60% involvement in nontraffic offenses by early adulthood (Christensen, 1967; Shannon, 1982; Wolfgang, 1977) and 22.8% involvement in serious offenses (Blumstein and Graddy,

1982). Even among the relatively high-risk cases studied by Robins (1966), only 60% of males were found to have been arrested and 36% had recorded arrests for serious (index) offenses.

Since the vast majority of the sample had both extensive juvenile records and a number of adult arrests, almost all were classified as chronic offenders (the base-rate for non-chronicity was quite low). The focus of the research changed, therefore, to differentiating *among* these chronic offenders in terms of the seriousness of their careers and to predicting variations in overall numbers of arrests (total and violent). Offenders were classified simply in terms of their most serious arrest (minor, property, violent-economic, or violent-aggressive).[1] While predictive analyses explained only a small portion (10–18%) of the variation in numbers of arrests, statistically significant differences were found among offender groups in terms of various background, attitudinal, and psychological variables. These findings suggested that for these serious delinquents, attitudinal and psychological differences did influence the overall intensity and seriousness of their adult criminal behavior; at the same time, much remained to be learned about these differences. Stability of the criminal behavior was not addressed; the loosely defined types were based on arrests covering the entire follow-up period. No attempt was made to investigate the usefulness of other typological distinctions or the usefulness of the obtained distinctions for characterizing careers over time.

The relatively large number of high-rate offenders in this sample, along with the fact that it was based on a prospective, longitudinal design, made it attractive for studying those issues related to development and change in offense careers over time. Half of this sample ($n = 1308$), along with smaller samples of adult offenders with no history of state-level commitments as juveniles, was used in the present study. More complete arrest-histories were obtained, and information on demographics, family background, adult drug use, marital status, and employment was coded from prison and/or probation files. These data allowed for extensive analysis of adult patterns of criminal behavior and the relationship of these patterns to various explanatory variables.

The Sample

The sample used for this study actually consisted of three separate subsamples, characterized by different levels of involvement with the criminal justice system. Although the bulk of the sample came from the above-mentioned studies involving California Youth Authority (CYA) wards, it was decided to broaden it somewhat by also including two additional samples of offenders: (a)

---

[1] A breakdown of the offenses included in these categories can be found at the end of this chapter.

a sample ($n = 175$) of adult prisoners who were convicted of robbery or burglary and who had no known history of state-level juvenile commitments (California Department of Corrections, or CDC, sample) and (b) a sample ($n = 98$) of adult probationers (Probation sample) who were sentenced to jail and/or probation for either robbery or burglary and who had, to that point, no prior juvenile or adult state-level commitments. Since some analyses focused on differences by sample, the CYA cases were also differentiated in terms of those who had adult prison sentences and those for whom adult probation data were obtained. For clarity, the non-CYA prison and probation samples were generally referred to as "supplementary" samples (e.g., supplementary CDC).

The Supplementary CDC sample was obtained by CDC data processing staff. The intent was to obtain a sample of 200 former prisoners who were similar to the former CYA wards, but who had no history of CYA (or similar) commitments. Since recent incapacitation research had focused primarily on robbers and burglars, the sample was limited to offenders who, at one time or another, were committed to prison for robbery or burglary. The data system at CDC did not contain information on juvenile commitments, so it was decided to select a much larger sample, check the names against the CYA files to determine prior CYA commitments, and then randomly select cases from among those with no such CYA experience. A computer program was written to randomly select 500 cases from among those former CDC inmates with the following characteristics:

- Male
- Convicted of robbery or burglary
- Born between 1946 and 1950
- Discharged or paroled in 1975 to 1977
- Paroled to a California location

Of those 500 cases, over 300 (60%) were found to have had prior CYA commitments.[2] As a result, the sample of potential CDC cases dropped to less than 200. Rather than request additional names, the decision was made to proceed with a slightly smaller sample than was originally planned. Additional attrition resulted from missing prison files and from some individuals having been returned to prison from parole and not finally discharged prior to the data collection (prison files were exceedingly difficult to obtain if cases were still "active," since they were kept at the institution or parole office to which the offender was assigned). The final supplementary CDC sample contained 175 cases.

---

[2] It was unclear whether this high proportion was due to a sampling fluke or, rather, was indicative of the contribution of former CYA wards to the population of robbers and burglars in CDC at that time. Time and resources did not permit following up on this interesting question.

Probation cases were more difficult to obtain, since counties generally do not have computer facilities that permit random sampling based on particular characteristics. Further, since probation files are typically retained only five years after the case is closed, the offender would have to have been arrested within the prior six or seven years. Offenders with serious offenses (robbery or burglary) and who were of similar age to the CYA cases (early thirties) but who had no prior CYA or prison experience were rare. Consequently, data collection was limited to Los Angeles County, which was large enough to provide more cases, and San Diego County, which did have some computer capability in this regard. Further, the inclusion criteria had to be relaxed somewhat, allowing younger offenders into the sample, and enabling some offenders who were not robbers or burglars to be selected (especially if they had a *prior* or *subsequent* offense of those kinds). Because these criteria changes made the probation sample less comparable to the remaining cases, and because considerable time and resources were required to obtain and code the data, a decision was made to limit the number of cases. A total of only 98 cases was obtained, but this number was felt to be large enough to permit identifying gross differences in the patterns of adult careers among the probationers, as compared to others.

The overall sample was *not* a representative sample of any particular offender group and certainly not representative of all offenders. Because of the restrictions placed on the sample before random selection, the supplementary cases (Probation or CDC) can only be held to represent cases like themselves: convicted as adults for robbery or burglary, male, born before 1950, etc. For the Probation cases, a somewhat broader sample was drawn, by necessity, but the representativeness of these cases of all probationers is unlikely. In contrast, since the CYA cases were drawn from institutions designed for both regular and serious wards, this part of the sample is reasonably representative of the types of cases handled by the CYA during that period. They may also be reasonably representative of all California offenders who began serious criminal careers early in life.

While the extent to which the offense rates and career patterns found for this sample can be generalized to other offenders in unknown, findings regarding general patterns and stability can be argued to have a general applicability. Most of the issues being addressed in this study were based on conceptions of criminal careers that should apply to *all offenders*. There is no reason to believe, for example, that offenders starting their careers early in life would have less stable adult careers than others. Thus, although this sample does not permit the drawing of conclusions about what *does* characterize criminal careers, in general, it is adequate for determining whether certain generalizations *do not* hold across the board. Further, no reason was found for believing that those general criminal career characteristics found for this sample of serious adult offenders could have been peculiar to these offenders. Nevertheless, such a possibility exists, and conclusions are, it is hoped, appropriately tempered.

TABLE 2.1 Subsamples included in various analyses

Analysis type	Report chapter	CYA ($n = 1308$)			Supplement	
		R/0[a]	Prob	CDC	Prob	CDC
N of cases (total = 1581)		674	142	492	98	175
Participation	3	*	*	*		
Aggregate arrest rates	4	*	*	*		
Methodological issues	5	*	*	*	*	*
Arrest-rate stability	6	*	*	*	*	*
Pre/post incarceration comparisons	7		*	*	*	*
Correlates and prediction of arrest rates	8		*	*	*	*
Incapacitation effects	9			*		*

[a] "Rap-sheet Only" cases: CYA cases with no adult prison terms and no recent probation reports.

In some instances, and for some analyses, of course, it was possible to assume some bias in the results based on sampling characteristics. For example, because the supplementary samples were chosen on the basis of known arrests for robbery or burglary, these cases would not be appropriate for studying either participation in various kinds of crimes or offense rates. Similarly, these subsamples would not be useful for studying the changes in participation or offense rates by age, since the sampling criteria increased the likelihood that robbery or burglary arrests would occur as adults and at particular times (in order for the CDC cases to be released between 1975 and 1977 and for the Probation cases to have active probation files). Consequently, only the CYA cases, who comprised a cohort identified (for the most part) prior to their becoming adults, were used in these analyses of participation and arrest rates, as they differ by race and age. Other analyses were also limited to various subsamples whenever it was reasoned that bias may have resulted from including others. The nature and bases for these restrictions will be discussed in the context of describing and presenting the findings of the particular analyses. A general guide to the subsamples that were included in various analysis is provided in Table 2.1.

The Data

Three sources of data were used. Information on criminal behavior was obtained primarily from California Criminal Identification and Investigation (CII) rap sheets. Background and lifestyle information came from adult prison file materials and from pre-sentence investigation (PSI) reports found in county probation files. These reports sometimes provided additional data on criminal behavior as well, since offenders were sometimes known to have committed crimes for which they were never arrested. Whenever possible, copies of the relevant file materials (cumulative summaries from CDC and PSI reports from probation) were obtained, rather than coded on site. This procedure facilitated double-checking of coding procedures, clarification of problems encountered during editing, and, importantly, the ability to continue the research in the future. Clues about the causes and correlates of criminal behavior or of changes in behavior patterns could be pursued in future studies without having to repeat the data collection. Of the 1308 CYA cases randomly selected for the sample, 634 (or 48%) had CDC or PSI data; the remainder had only rap sheet (arrest) data through 1985.

Note that since the data came from official sources, the most information was available for those offenders who had the most contact with the criminal justice system. Further, follow-up information on lifestyle factors for the CYA cases was limited to those individuals who either served terms in adult prison or for whom probation files (and thereby PSI reports) were available. Prison files are maintained in the CDC archives for 30 years, while probation reports were often not available, since probation departments typically destroy their inactive files after five years. As a result, relatively little information was available for the "successes" and for those offenders in the CYA sample who were never sent to prison and who were not placed on probation within the last six or seven years. For these cases, the data base was limited to official rap sheet information and data available from the earlier study. CDC or PSI information, useful for understanding differences among offenders, was available for all of the CDC and Probation samples.

The **follow-up period** was defined by the date of the last information collected Because of the time and expense involved in obtaining information, the data were considered complete for each case if criminal history data were available through 1980. Thus, every case with CDC or Probation information through 1980 was considered complete if that information included criminal history data. Rap sheets were ordered *only* for those cases with no CDC or Probation information and those cases for whom the CDC or Probation information did not extend through 1980. The date of the final data collection depended on the types and amounts of data available from CDC or Probation departments.

The Coding

To get the fullest picture of the likely criminal behavior of these offenders, offense data were coded to include every charge, count, and "cleared" crime noted on the rap sheet or written report. Separate entries were made for each type of crime and each date, so that multiple entries for the same date were possible. In a few instances, offenders were known to have committed a number of crimes for which they were not "charged" when arrested (e.g., a burglar may have committed a number of burglaries for which he was not formally charged as part of a plea bargain). These were coded as well, under the assumption that these indicators of overall criminality were probably no less valid than other officially recorded offense data. Thus, the data do not indicate the actual number of crimes for which each individual was apprehended. They also, obviously, do not indicate the actual number of crimes committed by these offenders; by and large, the present data can be expected to underestimate the actual levels of participation and rates of offending, although the extent of the bias is unknown. Further, disposition data were not coded, since it was usually impossible to determine the disposition of most counts or charges.

Other, "lifestyle" data were coded with respect to changes in status over the period covered in the CDC or probation report. Coded were changes in incarceration and supervision, known drug-use patterns, and marital and family status. Rules were established for coding ambiguous data. Each case was coded by one person and edited by another, who also reviewed the file materials. Any discrepancies or uncertainties concerning coding were discussed, and, if necessary, coding rules were refined. Even so, by the nature of the sources of the information, none of these data can be considered particularly valid or reliable as measures of the variables in question, although they indicate with reasonable accuracy the kinds of information available on offenders in CDC or recent probation reports.

The incarceration/supervision information came primarily from rap sheets. All time periods during the follow-up were coded, either as time "free," time under probation supervision, time in jail, time in prison, time under parole supervision, etc. Only the determination of jail time proved to be very problematic, since release dates generally were not available. Consequently, each jail term was coded as its sentence length unless the actual time served could be verified by the reports.

Drug use and marital status were coded in terms of changes in status. Offenders were assumed to maintain the same status unless the change was noted in the CDC or probation report. Although this assumption is questionable, and created a greater appearance of stability than was likely true for these offenders, no other assumption was possible. The types of drugs ever used as a juvenile and as an adult were also coded as separate variables.

Employment data were coded both in terms of the general pattern of employment for each calendar year from 1967 to 1984 and in terms of actual jobs noted in reports. Owing to the relatively few jobs, the inability to determine beginning and ending dates or the nature of the employment, the data on specific jobs was exceedingly difficult to code or interpret. The yearly data, although subjective and general, seemed to capture what was available in these reports fairly well. Coded were the number of months worked during each calendar year and the most common type of employment (e.g., full-time). If the individual did not work during a particular year because of disability or school enrollment, these situations were coded. This coding format was used primarily because entries in the records typically took that form (e.g., "Worked six months in 1975 as a part-time laborer").

One other kind of information was coded: data on the prison or jail/probation term for which the CDC or probation data were obtained. Where available, data were coded concerning background information on the offender and his family; the offense for which he was convicted; other offenses committed in the incident; entry, parole, and discharge dates; scholastic and aptitude test scores; psychological diagnoses; gang membership; and parole or probation information, including revocations. These data were used for assessing pre/post differences in types and numbers of arrests.

From these raw data, computer programs were used to generate monthly and yearly indices of crimes committed, incarceration time (prison and jail), "street" time (not incarcerated), drugs used, marital status, and employment. Most analyses, however, used data summarized by age. Calendar-year indices were transformed into indices by age on the basis of the age of each offender during each calendar year (the age he was during most of the year).[3]

These "age" data were used to create variables that allowed various analyses of the adult criminal careers:

- The entire adult career: age 18 to age 37 (or follow-up)
- Four-year age blocks: 18–21, 22–25, 26–29, 30–33, 34–37
- Even ages (18, 20, 22, etc.) and odd ages (19, 21, 23, etc.)

Separate files were created for the individuals who had probation data or who were sentenced to adult prison. These files contained the same data as other files, coded for those periods prior to and following the particular sentence for which the report was available. In cases where more than one report was available, the earliest sentence was used in order to maximize the amount of follow-up time after release from jail or prison.[4]

The Analyses

Most of the analyses of the data were performed using SPSSx, a common statistical package. The analytic methods were kept as simple as possible to maximize the clarity of the findings. Rather than describe all the various analyses at this point, each will be discussed in the context of presenting the

---

[3] With this method, offenders could have been as much as six months younger or older than their nominal "age" would indicate, and could have been as much as 11 or 12 months younger or older than others of the same "age." However, for the kinds of analyses performed, these differences from true ages were considered unimportant. The interest was in long-term trends and rather large (four-year) blocks of time, not in obtaining "true" estimates of offense rates or patterns of offending at specific ages.

[4] The data files are currently in the form of "system files" created using SPSSx (Statistical Package for the Social Sciences). They will be available from the Criminal Justice Archive and Information Network (University of Michigan, P.O. Box 1248, Ann Arbor, Michigan, 48106). Additional information can be obtained from the author.

findings. It was felt that this approach would help the reader to understand them better, and would free the reader from having to refer back to this chapter for clarification.

A few general observations, however, may be helpful. In a number of analyses, a distinction was made between cases who were "active" offenders and those who were not. As discussed in the introduction, assumptions about criminal careers generally refer to the "active" period: that period prior to the point where an offender drops out of crime completely. Although all members of the sample were, at one time or another, active in crime, it is unlikely that all of them continued to commit crimes throughout the years they were followed for the present study. While the data did not allow a clear determination of when these offenders had stopped committing crimes (since they may have continued to commit crimes without being arrested), it was deemed reasonable to assume that an offender who got arrested during a particular year was actively committing crimes during that year. Thus, it was assumed that each offender was active *at least* through the date of the last known arrest. Specifically, since the data were coded by calendar year, it was assumed that each offender was active through the year in which he was last arrested. The **active period** (or "known" active period) for each offender extended from the year he turned 18 to the year he was last arrested, and each offender was considered to have remained active throughout this active period (in analyses of arrest rates by age, the year of the last arrest was excluded—the procedure will be described fully later on). In other words, the offender was considered active until he committed his last crime (indicated in the present case by his last arrest), even if he stopped for several years or was incarcerated for a lengthy period.

In addition to the toal number of arrests (charges), most analyses used various combinations of crimes. For consistency, the offense groupings used in the earlier study involving these cases (Haapanen and Jesness, 1982) were used in this study as well. Offenses were categorized according to the following definitions:

Violent-aggressive—murder, rape, assault.
Violent-economic—robbery, other person offenses (extortion, kidnapping).
Violent—the above two types combined.
Property—burglary, receiving stolen property (RSP), grand theft, forgery, grand theft auto.
Serious—all violent and property offenses listed above (this category is somewhat comparable to FBI part 1 index offenses).

Chapter 3
Participation in Adult Crime among Former CYA Wards

As discussed earlier, offenders are committed to the California Youth Authority (CYA) because of serious and/or extensive involvement in criminality at an early age. Of those who were included in the present follow-up study, almost all (96%) apparently continued that involvement into adulthood (were arrested at least once).[1] The nature and extent of their involvement in adult criminal behavior, however, differed greatly among offenders: some were arrested only once or twice for minor offenses while others were arrested for as many as 40 different (often serious) crimes. In this chapter, some of these differences will be explored.[2]

Data on charged offenses over the follow-up period, extending into the early to mid-thirties for most cases, were analyzed to determine the kinds of crimes in which these offenders were believed to be involved, the extent and breadth of that involvement, the mix of crimes (variety vs. specialization), the prevalence of offenders charged more than once for particular offenses and combinations of offenses, and variations in participation by race and, for active offenders, by age. Findings for the sample as whole provide an indication of expected long-range criminal behavior patterns for offenders who engage in serious criminal behavior early in life. Of special interest, however, will be the differences along these dimensions by race and by age, since these differences have broader implications for evaluating current ideas about criminal careers and the assumptions underlying the concept of selective incapacitation.

In the analyses that follow, "participation" in particular crimes is defined as

---

[1] This high probability of engaging in criminal behavior as adults is consistent with the findings of numerous research studies that followed serious juvenile offenders into adulthood for varying lengths of time (Shannon, 1982; Farrington, 1983; Wolfgang, Thornberry, and Figlio, 1985). These studies (and others) are reviewed in Blumstein et al., (1986).

[2] As discussed in Chapter 2, these analyses will focus only on cases from the original CYA cohorts. Other cases were excluded from these analyses because they were selected for the study on the basis of having been convicted of particular kinds of offenses, making them inappropriate for studying levels of participation.

having been arrested at least once for that crime (or crime type) during the adult follow-up period.[3] In contrast, being "active" in crime is defined temporally; it is that time period prior to the date of the last known arrest. Offenders were considered active in crime as long as they were being arrested. "Active offenders" were all offenders who at particular points in time (say, a particular age) had not yet been arrested for the last time. This distinction will be discussed in more detail in the section focusing on age effects.

As outlined in Chapter 2, offenses were categorized according to the following definitions:

Violent-aggressive—homicide (murder 1st, murder 2nd, manslaughter), rape, assault.
Violent-economic—robbery, other person offenses (extortion, kidnapping).
Violent—the above two types combined.
Property—burglary, receiving stolen property (RSP), grand theft, forgery, grand theft auto (GTA).
Any Serious—all violent and property offenses listed above (this category is somewhat comparable to FBI part 1 index offenses).

Throughout this discussion, it will be important to keep in mind that because official data were used, estimates of participation in criminal activity will underestimate the actual levels of participation.

Types of Levels of Participation in Crime

This section will focus generally on the number of times these former CYA wards were arrested as adults for various crimes, for the total sample, and for each ethnic group separately. Analyses of the numbers of cases with arrests of various types suggest clear ethnic differences both in the proportions of cases participating in various crimes and in the extent of that participation.

Table 3.1 shows the frequency distributions and percentages participating at each level for general categories of offenses. The columns labeled Cum % show the percentage of the sample and each ethnic group with at least that many offenses of each type. These figures indicate, therefore, both the proportion of cases with *any* arrests of these types and the proportions with multiple arrests. For example, 56.6% of the total sample had one or more arrests for ("participated" in) violent-aggressive crimes, 44% participated in violent-economic crimes, 75.1% in property crimes, and so on.

---

[3] Having arrests is not a good indicator of participation, since many offenders who commit various crimes never get arrested for them. Nevertheless, since there has been no empirical evidence of substantial differences in arrest probability by race or age (Hindelang, 1978; Hindelang, Hirschi, and Weiss, 1979; Cohen, 1986), these data can be used to draw reasonable inferences about differences in participation by ethnicity and age.

TABLE 3.1 Number and percent with arrests for serious offenses by race.

Offense type	White (n = 713)		Black (n = 359)		Hispanic (n = 210)		Total[a] (n = 1282)	
	%	Cum%	%	Cum%	%	Cum%	%	Cum%
Violent-aggressive								
0	51.1%	100.0%	35.7%	100.0%	30.5%	100.0%	43.4%	100.0%
1	20.2%	48.9%	17.5%	64.3%	21.9%	69.5%	19.7%	56.6%
2	12.8%	28.8%	12.0%	46.8%	15.7%	47.6%	13.0%	36.9%
3	5.6%	16.0%	11.1%	34.8%	10.5%	31.9%	8.0%	23.9%
4	4.6%	10.4%	7.8%	23.7%	7.1%	21.4%	5.9%	15.9%
5 +	5.8%	5.8%	15.9%	15.9%	14.3%	14.3%	10.0%	10.0%
Violent-economic								
0	66.2%	100.0%	37.0%	100.0%	53.8%	100.0%	56.0%	100.0%
1	16.0%	33.8%	19.8%	63.0%	20.0%	46.2%	17.7%	44.0%
2	10.0%	17.8%	13.4%	43.2%	11.9%	26.2%	11.2%	26.3%
3	3.5%	7.8%	9.2%	29.8%	5.7%	14.3%	5.5%	15.1%
4	1.5%	4.3%	5.3%	20.6%	4.8%	8.6%	3.1%	9.6%
5 +	2.8%	2.8%	15.3%	15.3%	3.8%	3.8%	6.5%	6.5%
Property								
0	27.9%	100.0%	17.8%	100.0%	26.7%	100.0%	24.9%	100.0%
1	15.0%	72.1%	13.1%	82.2%	16.7%	73.3%	14.7%	75.1%
2	15.7%	57.1%	9.5%	69.0%	10.5%	56.6%	13.1%	60.4%
3	9.8%	41.4%	8.6%	59.5%	9.0%	46.1%	9.4%	47.3%
4	6.5%	31.6%	8.6%	50.9%	7.1%	37.1%	7.2%	37.9%
5 +	25.1%	25.1%	42.3%	42.3%	30.0%	30.0%	30.7%	30.7%
Any Serious								
0	16.3%	100.0%	7.8%	100.0%	11.0%	100.0%	13.0%	100.0%
1	10.1%	83.7%	7.2%	92.2%	7.1%	89.0%	8.8%	87.0%
2	10.1%	73.6%	3.9%	85.0%	10.0%	81.9%	8.3%	78.2%
3	11.5%	63.5%	7.2%	81.1%	7.1%	71.9%	9.6%	69.8%
4	7.6%	52.1%	2.8%	73.8%	5.7%	64.8%	5.9%	60.2%
5 +	44.5%	44.5%	71.0%	71.0%	59.0%	59.0%	54.3%	54.3%
Any violent								
0	39.3%	100.0%	18.9%	100.0%	20.5%	100.0%	30.5%	100.0%
1	18.5%	60.8%	14.5%	81.0%	15.2%	79.5%	16.8%	69.5%
2	13.5%	42.3%	8.6%	66.5%	14.8%	64.3%	12.3%	52.7%
3	9.1%	28.8%	10.6%	57.9%	11.4%	49.5%	9.9%	40.4%
4	6.9%	19.7%	7.2%	47.3%	14.8%	38.1%	8.3%	30.5%
5 +	12.8%	12.8%	40.1%	40.1%	23.3%	23.3%	22.2%	22.2%

[a]Cases not classified as white, Hispanic, or black (n = 26) were excluded.

The figures in this table reinforce the notion that this was a very high-risk sample of offenders. Not only were almost all offenders arrested at one time or another as adults, but the vast majority were arrested for serious crimes, with three-quarters of the sample being arrested for a serious property crime. Participation in violent crimes was somewhat lower, but still included over two-thirds of the sample. Participation in specific categories of violent crimes was also very high.

The figures in Table 3.1 also indicate that repetitiveness was relatively common among these offenders. Over two-thirds of the sample had three or more charges for serious offenses during the follow-up period (this amounts to 80.2% of all those with any serious charges), with half the sample accumulating at least five such charges. The percentage of cases with three or more violent-aggressive or violent-economic offenses was not as high (24% and 15%, respectively), but when all violent offenses were combined, four in ten had at

TABLE 3.2 Number and percent participating in each offense type by race.

	White (n = 713)		Black (n = 359)		Hispanic (n = 210)		Total[a] (n = 1282)	
Offense type	No.	%	No.	%	No.	%	No.	%
Violent-aggressive								
Homicide	45	6.3%	32	8.9%	22	10.5%	99	7.7%
Agg. assault	254	35.6%	189	52.6%	114	54.3%	557	43.4%
Rape	36	5.0%	39	10.9%	13	6.2%	88	6.9%
Misd. assault	157	22.0%	98	27.3%	68	32.4%	323	25.2%
Violent-economic								
Armed robbery	135	18.9%	121	33.7%	55	26.2%	311	24.3%
Strongarm robbery	135	18.9%	166	46.2%	62	29.5%	363	28.3%
Other person	71	10.0%	63	17.5%	21	10.0%	155	12.1%
Property								
Burglary	379	53.2%	237	66.0%	130	61.9%	746	58.2%
Rec. stolen prop.	241	33.8%	162	45.1%	66	31.4%	469	36.6%
Grand theft	143	20.1%	118	32.9%	50	23.8%	311	24.3%
Forgery	152	21.3%	82	22.8%	26	12.4%	260	20.3%
Grand theft auto	125	17.5%	86	24.0%	34	16.2%	245	19.1%
Other Offenses								
Arson	15	2.1%	12	3.3%	5	2.4%	32	2.5%
Other theft	265	37.2%	144	40.1%	87	41.4%	496	38.7%
Joyride	179	25.1%	116	32.3%	41	19.5%	336	26.2%
Weapons offenses	220	30.9%	170	47.4%	68	32.4%	458	35.7%
Sex offenses	87	12.2%	58	16.2%	17	8.1%	162	12.6%
Liquor offenses	290	40.7%	107	29.8%	134	63.8%	531	41.4%
Drug use	395	55.4%	224	62.4%	144	68.6%	763	59.5%
Drug sales	84	11.8%	38	10.6%	38	18.1%	160	12.5%
Other offenses	606	85.0%	297	82.7%	186	88.6%	1089	84.9%

[a] Cases not classified as white, Hispanic, or black (n = 26) were excluded.

least three charged offenses. This figure is only slightly lower than the percentage with three or more property offenses.

Among these former serious juvenile offenders, differences in adult participation by race, although not as marked as for the general population, were still evident. The ratio of participation in violent crimes by minorities to that of whites was around 1.3:1. The largest difference was for violent-economic crimes, where black participation exceeded white participation by a factor of almost 1.9:1. The black-white ratio for participation in any serious offense was 1.1:1, which is strikingly different from the estimated ratio of 3.6:1 for index offenses in the general population reported by Blumstein and Graddy (1982). The *distributions* of offenses also show clear differences by ethnicity; whites generally had lower levels of involvement, especially for violent crimes. The proportion of whites with five or more violent crimes, for example, was one-third that of blacks and around half that for Hispanics. Blacks showed higher levels of involvement in each crime type.

Participation rates for selected specific offenses are shown in Table 3.2, and the rates for specific serious offenses are displayed graphically in Figure 3.1 for the three ethnic groups. For the total sample, participation rates were at or above 25% for 11 of the 21 types of offenses considered. An additional three offenses had participation rates at or above 20%. Except for such low-base-rate offenses as homicide, rape, and arson, all other offenses had participation rates above 10%. The highest rates of participation were for miscellaneous ("other") offenses and drug-use offenses, but the next two most common

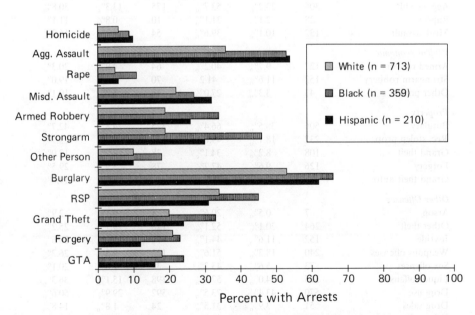

FIGURE 3.1 Percent participating in various crimes by race.

offenses were the relatively serious crimes of burglary (58.2%) and aggravated assault (43.4%). Thus, for offenders initiating serious criminal careers at an early age, the chances of being arrested for most of the offenses listed was over 20%, with the chances of being arrested for burglary or aggravated assault closer to 50/50.

Although the differences were mostly small, blacks showed the highest participation rates for most of the offenses listed, especially for sex offenses and property offenses. Blacks generally showed lower participation rates for liquor offenses and drug offenses. Hispanics had the highest rates of participation in aggressive violent crimes (except rape) and in drug or alcohol-related crimes, while showing lower rates of participation in forgery, auto theft, and sex offenses. Whites had the lowest participation rates for most offenses, but the difference was substantial only for aggravated assault and robbery.

TABLE 3.3 Number and percent of multiple offenders for each offense type.

	Two or more offenses			Three or more offenses		
Offense	N	% of Sample	% of Participants	N	% of Sample	% of Participants
No multiple arrests	144	11.0%		291	22.2%	
Violent-aggressive						
Homicide	17	1.3%	16.5%	6	0.5%	5.8%
Agg. assault	305	23.2%	53.7%	175	13.3%	30.8%
Rape	28	2.1%	31.1%	10	0.8%	11.1%
Misd. assault	132	10.1%	39.6%	54	4.1%	16.2%
Violent-economic						
Armed robbery	127	9.7%	40.2%	64	4.9%	20.3%
Strongarm robbery	152	11.6%	41.2	70	5.3%	19.0%
Other person	43	3.3%	27.0%	16	1.2%	10.1%
Property						
Burglary	506	38.5%	66.4%	325	24.8%	42.7%
Rec. stolen prop.	237	18.1%	49.6%	123	9.4%	25.7%
Grand theft	108	8.2%	34.1%	38	2.9%	12.0%
Forgery	126	9.6%	47.7%	78	5.9%	29.5%
Grand theft auto	86	6.5%	34.7%	47	3.6%	19.0%
Other Offenses						
Arson	7	0.5%	20.6%	1	0.1%	2.9%
Other theft	264	20.1%	52.1%	128	9.7%	25.2%
Joyride	152	11.6%	44.1%	71	5.4%	20.6%
Weapons offenses	240	18.3%	51.6%	122	9.3%	26.2%
Sex offenses	73	5.6%	43.2%	34	2.6%	20.1%
Liquor offenses	315	24.0%	57.8%	198	15.1%	36.3%
Drug use	570	43.4%	73.5%	392	29.9%	50.6%
Drug sales	51	3.9%	31.5%	24	1.8%	14.8%
Other offenses	945	72.0%	31.5%	787	59.9%	70.6%

Table 3.3 shows the number of multiple offenders within each specific crime.[4] Shown are the number of cases with two or more arrests for each offense and the number with three or more arrests. These figures are also shown both as a percentage of the entire sample of CYA cases (% of Sample) and as a percentage of those cases with at least one arrest of that kind (% of Participants). For example, there were 17 offenders who were arrested two or more times for homicide (murder or manslaughter); these 17 cases constituted 1.3% of all cases in the sample and 16.5% of all offenders who were arrested at least once for a homicide offense. Of those 17 cases, six were arrested *three* or more times; these six cases were 0.5% of the sample and 5.8% of all cases ever arrested (as adults) for homicide.

Overall, the data indicate that being charged with two or more offenses of a single type was not a common occurrence in this sample of offenders. Other than arrests for miscellaneous "other" offenses, drug use was the most common offense resulting in multiple arrests, followed by burglary, liquor offenses and aggravated assault. These four offense types were also by far the most common crimes for which offenders were arrested three or more times. Multiple arrests for homicide, rape, other person offenses, arson, sex offenses, and (interestingly) drug sales, on the other hand, were rare, especially at the level of three or more charged offenses.

When only the percent of *participants* in each type of crime who had multiple charges is considered, the extent of repetition appears more substantial. In most cases, the likelihood of an offender having more than one arrest was over 30%, with repetition for aggravated assault, burglary, receiving stolen property, theft, weapons offenses and drug use and liquor offenses near or above 50%. In general, these percentages were higher than the percentages of the sample with any participation in these crimes, suggesting some tendency to repeat crimes. For example, of the 162 cases (12.6% of the sample) who were ever arrested for a sex offense other than rape (Table 3.2), 73 (or 43.2%) had at least two such offenses and $34/73 = 46.6\%$ of those with at least two arrests had three or more. Thus, while the probability of ever being charged with a sex offenses was 12.6% in this sample, the probability of being charged for a *second* offense, given the first, increased to 43.2%. Once arrested for a second sex offense, the probability of being arrested at least one more time for the same offense was 46.6%. These subsequent offenses, however, may not have been the *next* offense—the offender may have been arrested for a number of other crimes before being charged with another sex offense.

---

[4] These figures are not broken down by ethnicity because of the small number of multiple offenders for most crimes; consequently, cases in the "other" category of race were also included. In addition, no distinction was made between cases who were actually *arrested* on more than one occasion for the crime in question and those who were arrested once and *charged* with multiple counts. Both indicate repetitive involvement in the crime. The terms "multiple arrests" and "multiple charges" will be used interchangeably in this context.

TABLE 3.4 Number and percent of arrests for types of offenses by race.

Offense type	White (n = 713)	Black (n = 359)	Hispanic (n = 210)	Total (n = 1282)
Total	11510	7344	4212	23066
Mean:	16.1	20.5	20.1	18.0
Violent-aggressive	831	790	428	2049
	7.2%	10.8%	10.2%	8.9%
Violent-economic	521	729	212	1462
	4.5%	9.9%	5.0%	6.3%
Property	2332	1675	757	4764
	20.3%	22.8%	18.0%	20.7
Other offenses	7826	4150	2815	14791
	68.0%	56.5%	66.8%	64.1%
Total violent	1352	1519	640	3511
	11.7%	20.7%	15.2%	15.2%
Total felony	3684	3194	1397	8275
	32.0%	43.5%	33.2%	35.9%

Types of Crimes as a Proportion of the Total

Members of the three ethnic groups also differed with respect to the relative proportions of various offenses making up the total array of arrests. This breakdown, for the general categories of crimes, is shown in Table 3.4, and displayed graphically in Figure 3.2. Since the table also shows the total number of crimes of each type, the sheer volume of crimes charged against

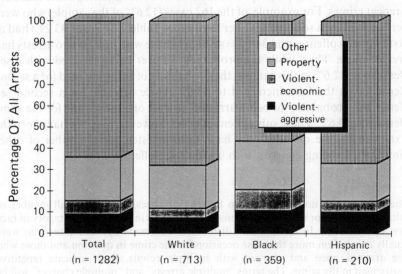

FIGURE 3.2 Arrests for various types of crimes as a percentage of the total by race.

these offenders is readily apparent. The 1282 offenders in this sample (excluding "other" ethnicities) were charged with over 23,000 crimes as adults, for an average of 18 crimes apiece. This average differs, once again, by race, with whites averaging four fewer charged crimes per case than blacks or Hispanics. About two-thirds of these offenses, however, were of relatively minor nature. Of the serious offenses, most were for property crimes (20.7% of all crimes, and 57.6% of all serious offenses). Serious violent crimes were evenly divided between those of an aggressive nature and those of a more economic nature.

Blacks had a higher proportion of all three major types of serious crimes and a consequently lower proportion of more minor offenses than whites or Hispanics. The proportion of violent-economic offenses, for example, was twice as high for blacks as for others. Although whites and Hispanics had about the same overall proportion of serious crimes among their charged offenses, Hispanics had a higher proportion of violent-aggressive offenses and a lower proportion of property offenses.

Breadth of Involvement

Such analyses suggested that these serious offenders participated in a variety of offenses, with participation rates for both violent offenses and property offenses above 50%. Moreover, although the majority of offenses were minor, the proportion of various violent offenses and property offenses was substantial. The question arises as to whether these overall proportions were the result of different offenders committing different types of crime more-or-less exclusively or, rather, the result of all offenders committing a variety of crimes.

To assess the extent of variability/specialization in the careers of these offenders, each offender was classified in terms of the different types of serious crimes appearing on his arrest record.[5] To establish overall levels of involvement in more than one type of serious offense, these analyses were first performed for all cases. To better assess the extent of *specialization* in this sample, the analysis was repeated, including only those cases with at least three serious charges; cases with fewer than three arrests were excluded because those with only one arrest are, by necessity, specialists (and cases with two serious arrests are limited to two types). The results of these analyses are presented in Table 3.5.

As shown in the table, 27.9% of all cases in the sample were charged at least once for each of the three major types of serious crimes (these offenders constitute 32% of all cases with any serious charges). Adding together the

---

[5] The interest here was primarily in serious crimes; involvement in minor crimes was so high (over 94% for all three ethnic groups) that virtually all these offenders would have arrests for minor crimes in addition to their more serious arrests.

TABLE 3.5 Participation in multiple serious offense groups by race.

Offense combination	White	Black	Hispanic	Total
All Cases				
N of cases	713	359	210	1282
None	16.3%	7.8%	11.0%	13.0%
Property only	23.0%	11.1%	9.5%	17.5%
Violent-economic only	1.3%	2.2%	1.9%	1.6%
Violent-aggressive only	7.6%	4.2%	10.0%	7.0%
Property/Violent-economic	10.5%	14.5%	8.1%	11.2%
Property/Violent-aggressive	19.4%	13.9%	23.3%	18.5%
Violent-econ./Violent-agg.	2.8%	3.6%	3.8%	3.2%
All Three	19.2%	42.6%	32.4%	27.9%
Cases with 3 + Serious				
N of cases	453	291	151	895
Property only	20.1%	6.9%	7.3%	13.6%
Violent-economic only	.2%	.7%	.7%	.4%
Violent-aggressive only	2.6%	1.7%	3.3%	2.5%
Property/Violent-economic	15.5%	17.2%	10.6%	15.2%
Property/Violent-aggressive	28.0%	16.5%	29.1%	24.5%
Violent-econ./Violent-agg.	3.3%	4.5%	4.0%	3.8%
All three	30.2%	52.6%	45.0%	40.0%

percentages for the four categories indicating involvement in at least two types of crimes, a total of 60.8% of all cases (or 70% of all cases charged with any serious offenses) had charges in at least two groups. Together, the offenders with arrests for only one type of crime (specialists) constituted only 26.1% of the sample, making specialization less likely than being a three-type offender. Offenders with charges for only one type of violent crime were especially rare, constituting only 8.6% of the total sample.

Even among *participants* in each type of crime, specialization was low (these figures are not shown in Table 3.5). Specialization among participants was determined by dividing the percentage of the sample who committed only one type of crime by the total number of cases who were ever arrested for that crime (participants). For example, 75.1% (from Table 3.1) of the sample were involved in property crimes, and 17.5% of the sample were involved *only* in property crimes. Among these participants in property crimes, only 23.3% (17.5/75.1 × 100) were specialists: 76.7% were also involved in violent crimes. Comparable figures for specialists in violent-aggressive and violent-economic crimes are 3.6% and 12.4% respectively.[6] Such a lack of specialization in

---

[6] This is a somewhat different approach to studying specialization than has been used in other research, which has focused on the likelihood that a given arrest will be for the same crime as the previous arrest (Wolfgang et al., 1972; Bursik, 1980; Smith and Smith, 1984). Because of the large numbers of arrests averaged by these offenders, overall tendencies to commit certain types of crimes seemed a more appropriate way to characterize total careers.

violent crimes is not surprising, given the high participation rate for property crimes, but specialization in property crimes was also low in this sample.

The extent of *variety* in the offense types of these offenders can be seen in the proportion of participants in each type of crime who showed charges for *all three types* of serious crimes. Computations similar to those above show that $27.9/56.6 \times 100$, or 49.3% of all participants in violent-aggressive crimes were involved in all three types of crimes. Over half (63.4%) of those ever charged with a violent-economic crime were charged as well with both property and violent-agressive crimes. Among property offenders, 37.2% were three-type offenders. Considering that some portion of the sample had only one or two serious arrests in all (and were therefore not able to achieve the three-type distinction), these figures suggest a general tendency for offenders to distribute their crimes among offense types.

Turning to the bottom part of Table 3.5, one can see that among the 895 offenders with three or more serious charges, four in ten were three-typers, with the others spread fairly evenly among property crime specialists and combinations of property crimes and violent crimes. Summing across percentages shows that virtually all offenders with three or more serious charges (93.3%) had at least one property crime charged against them. Conversely, only 6.7% were charged exclusively with violent crimes.

The figures for the different ethnic groups indicate that whites in this sample were much more likely than others to specialize in property crimes, particularly at the higher level of criminality. They were also less likely to be generalists than either blacks or Hispanics. Between the two minority groups, Hispanics were somewhat less likely to have all three types of crimes in their records, but more likely to have a property/violent-aggressive combination. A higher proportion of blacks fell into the property/violent-economic category. These findings are consistent with the findings presented earlier, which showed blacks to have higher levels of participation in robbery and property crimes, while Hispanics had higher levels of participation in violent-aggressive crimes, such as assault. The higher involvement of blacks in robbery is also consistent with other research (Hindelang, 1978; Hindelang, Hirschi, and Weiss, 1979; Cohen, 1986).

To identify cases with extensive involvement in various combinations of crimes, the typology was then restricted to cases with two or more arrests per type of crime and to those with three or more arrests per type. These results are shown in Table 3.6. These figures show that over 75% of the sample had two or more charges in at least one type of offense (over 60% had three or more charges for one type of crime and/or another). Again, the vast majority of these cases were extensively involved in property crimes. Eleven percent of the cases in this sample had at least two arrest charges in each of the three major categories of crime.

Adding various categories, it was found that over 20% of the sample had two or more charged offenses for both property and violent-economic crimes (property/violent-economic + all three). Over one in four had two or more

TABLE 3.6 Participation in multiple serious offense groups by race: Multiple arrests in each group.

Offense combination	White (n = 713)	Black (n = 359)	Hispanic (n = 210)	Total (n = 1282)
2 + Arrests per Type				
None	30.0%	16.7%	22.4%	25.0%
Property only	31.7%	19.8%	18.6%	26.2%
Violent-economic only	2.7%	3.9%	2.9%	3.0%
Violent-aggressive only	7.6%	6.4%	15.7%	8.6%
Property/Violent-economic	6.9%	12.8%	8.6%	8.8%
Property/Violent-aggressive	12.9%	13.9%	17.1%	13.9%
Violent-econ./Violent-agg.	2.7%	3.9%	2.4%	3.0%
All three	5.6%	22.6%	12.4%	11.5%
3 + Arrests per Type				
None	47.8%	24.5%	36.2%	39.4%
Property only	30.9%	25.1%	21.9%	27.8%
Violent-economic only	2.1%	4.5%	2.4%	2.8%
Violent-aggressive only	7.3%	8.4%	14.3%	8.7%
Property/Violent-economic	3.2%	11.1%	7.6%	6.2%
Property/Violent-aggressive	6.2%	12.3%	13.3%	9.0%
Violent-econ./Violent-agg.	1.4%	3.1%	1.0%	1.8%
All three	1.1%	11.1%	3.3%	4.3%

charges for both property and violent-aggressive offenses. While only 4.3% of the sample had at least three offenses in each of the three types, over 10% had that level of involvement in both property and violent-economic crimes, with 13% being charged with three or more property and violent-aggressive offenses.

As with earlier findings, blacks showed more extensive involvement in combinations of offenses involving property and violent crimes: almost 50% had two or more property crimes *and* violent crimes of one type or the other charged against them, and over 22% had two or more charges for each of the three major types of offenses. Over one-third (37.6%) of the blacks in the sample were involved in two or more crime types at the level of three or more offenses each; the proportions for whites and Hispanics were 11.9% and 25.2%, respectively. Whites again showed the lowest levels of multiple, extensive involvement. The percentage of whites involved in all three types of crimes at the level of two or more charges each was about one-fourth that of blacks (5.6% vs. 22.6%) and one-tenth at the level of three or more offenses (1.1% vs. 11.1%).

Thus, broad, extensive involvement in criminality was more common among the minorities in this sample, particularly among the black members. These differences suggest that factors associated with race affect not only the likelihood of engaging in criminal behavior of the types studied here,[7] but also the nature and extent of involvement in these crimes. Even though all the members of the sample had histories of serious criminal behavior at an early age, differences in the nature of their adult criminal involvement were evident. The findings suggest that factors associated with race continued to have an influence on criminality throughout the careers of these young offenders.

Patterns of Participation by Age

A common theme in criminological literature is that criminal involvement differs by age (Blumstein et al., 1986; Hirschi and Gottfredson, 1983; Greenberg, 1985; Farrington, 1986). The population arrest rate has generally been found to "peak" during the late teens and early twenties and decline thereafter, so that a greater proportion of the population of 18 year olds gets arrested every year than of 35 year olds. Further, some offenders commit only one or two crimes during their teens and then quit entirely, while other offenders continue to engage in criminal behavior well into their fifties and sixties (West and Wright, 1981). Consequently, some portion of the 30-year-old arrestees were arrested for the first time at a much younger age. Some scholars consider an understanding of the factors that lead to continued criminal behavior over time (or, conversely, to "dropping out" from crime) to be among the most important tasks for research on criminal careers (Petersilia, 1980).

The foregoing analyses and findings have made clear that among the members of the present sample, continued criminal involvement as adults was both extensive and varied. This section will focus specifically on such issues as *how long* and to what extent they continued their criminal involvement as they got older. One type of analysis focused on the rate at which these offenders apparently dropped out of crime altogether—the proportion of cases who experienced their last known arrest during or after particular ages (remained "active" in crime through those ages). Other analyses investigated whether those offenders who remained active in crime committed fewer crimes as they got older.

Recent explanations of the declining arrest rate by age in the general population—and in most cross-sectional research on crime—have suggested that the decline is due mostly, if not entirely, to offenders "dropping out" of crime completely (Blumstein et al., 1986; Farrington, 1986). This conclusion is based on research that suggested that aggregate rates of criminal behavior remain constant throughout the period of active participation in crime (Blumstein and Cohen, 1979; Cohen, 1986). If this hypothesis holds for the types of serious offenders in this sample, one would expect to find particular

---

[7] Racial differences in the likelihood of ever engaging in criminal behavior could not, of course, be evaluated with the present sample of *offenders*, but has been supported by considerable research (see Blumstein et al., 1986).

relationships between age and various indices of criminal behavior. First, it would be expected that the proportion of cases actively participating in crime would decline substantially with age. Second, one would expect that of those cases known to be active in crime, a constant proportion would be arrested at each age. Third, the offense rates of "active" offenders would also be expected to remain stable over time. The last of these hypotheses will be addressed in the next chapter. The present analyses focused on the first two: the proportion of cases remaining active in crime through various ages and the proportion of "active" offenders with arrests during each age.

Continued participation was estimated by starting with cases who had their last known arrest after (i.e., were active at) age 21 and calculating the proportion who continued to be active through later ages. The interest was in determining the proportion of cases (among those active at age 21) who could still reasonably be considered active at each later age. While it seemed reasonable to assume that any individual who was arrested after a given age was still active at that age, the converse was not so easy to assume. The issue was how long an individual had to be arrest-free after a particular age before it could be reasonably assumed that he had actually dropped out of crime. Since no firm estimates were available from other research, it was decided (somewhat arbitrarily) that a period of three years was sufficient for assuming that no additional arrests would occur. In addition, it was required that this three-year follow-up period include at least 12 months of time on the street, to avoid considering an offender a "drop-out" simply because he spent three years in prison or jail. Thus, at each age, the sample included all cases with at least three years of follow-up, including at least 12 months of street time. Cases with any arrests at that age or later were considered "active" at that age, while those with no subsequent arrests were, by implication, assumed to have ended their criminal careers. The results up through age 32 are shown in Table 3.7.

As shown, there was a steady decline in the proportion of cases who, according to the above definition, remained active at various ages. For example, of those 1151 offenders who were active at age 21, 768 were followed at least through age 30, and thereby were included in the analysis for age 27. Of these 768 offenders, 563 (73.3%) were still active (had at least one arrest at age 27 or at some later age). By age 32, half the cases with three years of additional follow-up were still active in crime. Bearing in mind that these figures are conservative, since some "active" offenders may simply have been able to avoid arrest during those three years, these data suggest a high rate of persistence in criminal behavior for these offenders.

However, these "active" offenders did not necessarily have an arrest at *each* age. In fact, one would expect that some offenders at each age would show no arrests, if for no other reason that some portion of the sample was usually incarcerated. As discussed above, offense-rate stability implies that constant proportion of those cases who were active in crime and who were capable of being arrested (i.e., on the street) would be arrested at each age. This issue was investigated for the present sample by taking all the cases known to be

TABLE 3.7 Percent of active offenders at age 21
who remained active at later ages.

Age	N of cases[a]	Number active[b]	Percent active
21	1151	1151	100.0%
22	1118	1094	97.9%
23	1061	1006	94.8%
24	1001	902	90.1%
25	938	794	84.6%
26	861	678	78.7%
27	768	563	73.3%
28	658	456	69.3%
29	567	361	63.7%
30	518	299	57.7%
31	431	230	53.4%
32	261	127	48.7%

[a] Number of cases who were active at age 21 and who
had at least three years of follow-up beyond the age of
interest (including 12 + months of street time).
[b] Number of cases with an arrest at that age or later.

active at each age and calculating both the percent who were incarcerated the
full 12 months of that year and the percent with arrests at that age. Note that
here a slightly different operational definition of "active" was used. Since the
interest was simply in those cases known to still be active in crime, cases were
no longer required to have three years of follow-up beyond a given age. Being
active in crime was evidenced simply by having at least one arrest *after* the age
being considered. The "after" requirement ensured that the arrest that defined
each case as an active offender was not included in the analysis; the inclusion of
these "defining" arrests would bias the results upward, since each offender had
one. Consequently, the analysis involved only those ages for each offender
falling prior to the age at which the last known arrest occurred.

Shown in Table 3.8 are the number of cases who were active at each age, by
the above definition, whether they were on the street at that age or not. Also
shown are the number and percent of these active cases who spent that whole
year in prison or jail (to be active, these cases had to have been subsequently
released and then re-arrested). The final three columns of the table show the
number of active cases with any street time during that year and the percent of
those cases who were arrested at least once for any crime and, separately, for
any violent crime.

These percentages all show decreases over time. The percentage of the active
cases who were incarcerated rose over the ages 20 to 24 from 11.4% up to a
high of 16%. After age 24, this percentage dropped to around 8% by age 28, at
which point it leveled off. Among those offenders who were on the street at
least part of each year, there was a slight decline over time both in the
percentage arrested for any crime and in the percentage arrested for a violent

TABLE 3.8 Percent of nonincarcerated active offenders arrested at each age.

Age	Total active cases[a]	Incarcerated entire year		Any street time		
		N	%	N	% With any arrests	% With violent arrests
20	1180	135	11.4%	1045	64.8%	18.3%
21	1152	143	12.4%	1009	62.5%	17.2%
22	1107	146	13.2%	961	60.1%	17.0%
23	1041	146	14.0%	895	56.9%	17.0%
24	961	154	16.0%	807	52.9%	14.0%
25	866	123	14.2%	743	53.0%	14.7%
26	756	82	10.8%	674	47.6%	11.6%
27	537	52	08.2%	585	44.4%	13.5%
28	524	41	7.8%	483	46.4%	11.0%
29	405	32	7.9%	373	45.8%	10.2%
30	328	26	7.9%	302	44.4%	16.0%
31	254	16	6.3%	238	44.1%	16.1%
32	204	16	7.8%	188	37.2%	11.2%
33	142	12	8.5%	130	41.5%	12.3%

[a] Number of cases who were active at age 21 and who were active (had at least one arrest) *after* the age being analyzed.

crime. Starting from a high of 64.8% arrested at age 20, the percentage dropped more-or-less steadily to a low of 37.2% at age 32. The percentage of active offenders arrested for a violent crime also decreased somewhat over time, dropping from 18.3% at age 20 to 10.2% at age 29; at that point, the percentage jumped up to 16% for ages 30 and 31, before dropping once again to around 11% at age 32. Both percentages show a slight rise after age 32. Although the overall (any arrest) rate appears to decline faster, the percentage arrested at age 33 as a proportion of the percentage arrested at age 20 is only slightly lower for any arrest than for violent arrests (.57 vs. .61). The clear, though small, rise in these percentages in the late twenties (for any arrest) and around age 30 (for violent arrests) will be seen again in the next chapter, when aggregate offense rates by age are presented. Their meaning, however, is not clear at the present time.

Together, these two analyses show a pattern of declining criminal participation over time for these offenders. As they got older, more and more of these former serious delinquents dropped out of crime. Further, among those that remained actively involved, fewer and fewer were arrested each year, although the decline was not particularly steep. The latter finding may suggest that criminality did not decline much for these active offenders as they got older. However, it will be shown in the next chapter that while overall participation seemed to decline only slightly, the *rate* at which those offenders were arrested declined more dramatically as they aged.

Chapter 4
Adult Arrest Rates of Former CYA Wards

This chapter will focus on offense rates, as these are estimated from charged crimes in official records. Again, the interest will be primarily in differences in these rates by race and age. The data presented in the last chapter showed that participation in various crimes and combinations of crimes differed for ethnic groups in the sample and that participation declined with age for these offenders. In the present analyses, differences were also found in *rates* at which ethnic groups were arrested (number of arrests per year of time at risk—"street time") and in the rates at which these offenders were arrested at various ages.

In summarizing the existing literature on racial differences in offense rates, Cohen (1986) observes that the large differences in black and white rates of participation in crimes is not paralleled by large differences in the rates at which active offenders commit crimes. Racial differences, she suggests, appear to be largely a matter of differences in the proportions of each ethnic group that commit any crimes. Among active offenders, different ethnic groups are argued not to differ substantially in their rates of arrest (Blumstein and Cohen, 1979; Cohen, 1986). Further, some researchers have suggested that, while arrest rates in the general population may decline with age, these rates do not decline appreciably during periods of active involvement in crime—that arrest rates do not decline with age as long as offenders remain active in crime. For both arguments (minimal racial differences and no decline with age), the appropriate focus of investigation is argued to be "active" offenders: offenders who have not yet retired from crime. Further, the arguments concerning age effects focus on rates for specific offenses among active offenders who have committed those particular crimes. Individuals who have been arrested at least once for robbery in their lives (robbers), for example, can be expected to continue being arrested for robberies at the same rate until they stop getting arrested altogether. The present sample of adult offenders, with its high incidence of cases who remained active for a long period and its high participation rates for most offenses, can be used to assess the validity of these assertions.

As in the research cited above, the rates used in the present analyses were calculated on an aggregate level (all crimes divided by all accumulated street time for particular groups or for all offenders at particular ages). As such, these rates will have implications primarily for comparing groups. It will be important to keep in mind that the data refer to rates of *arrest*, rather than rates of committing crimes, but differences in these rates should reflect differences in actual offense rates. Some charged crimes were actually not committed by the individual so charged, and it is likely that many crimes were committed that never resulted in arrests. Since no adequate method was available for assessing either the extent of false charges in the records or the number of actual crimes committed, no attempt was made to estimate actual offense rates using the present data.[1] However, there has been little in the way of empirical evidence suggesting *differences* in arrest probability associated with race or age (Hindelang, 1978; Hindelang, Hirschi, and Weiss, 1979; Cohen, 1986); therefore, it should be possible to draw reasonable inferences about differences in offense rates from these analyses of arrest rates.

Following the format used in the previous chapter, data on arrest rates for those members of the CYA sample who are white, black, or Hispanic will be presented first.[2] The discussion will then turn to the findings concerning variation in these rates by age, both for the total sample and by ethnicity.

Arrest Rates over the Follow-up Period

Arrest rates were calculated for general categories of offenses and for specific offenses as the aggregate rate of arrest per year of street time for the entire sample and by race (again, the 26 cases not classified as white, black, or Hispanic were excluded). Each rate was calculated for all cases and then separately for "active participants," as described below.

First, the yearly rates of arrest (for each ethnic group) across *all CYA cases*, using all accumulated street time during the follow-up period were calculated. The numerator in these rates was simply the number of arrests occurring during the follow-up period; the denominator was the number of street years accumulated by all cases together during this period (cases could contribute partial years to the total). This analysis provided an indication of what might be expected in terms of overall differences in offense behavior for such a sample

---

[1] Although it is theoretically possible to infer actual offense rates from data on arrests, using estimates of the probability of arrest for various crimes (Blumstein and Cohen, 1979; Cohen, 1983, 1986), these estimated probabilities vary considerably across jurisdictions, types of crime, and types of offenders. Consequently, the applicability of various estimates of arrest probabilities to the present sample is highly uncertain.

[2] These aggregate rates will mask differences among sample members in the rates at which they get arrested or commit crimes. The pooled estimates for ethnic groups are merely "average" rates and are not meant to apply to individual offenders. It should be kept in mind that there was considerable variation in the rate at which *individual offenders* in this sample committed crimes.

of serious youthful offenders followed (in most cases) into their thirties. These rates will underestimate, however, the actual arrest rates for offenders who participated in various crimes, since nonparticipants contributed to the aggregate street-time figures. They will also underestimate the actual rates of arrest occurring while offenders were actively committing crimes, since street time after "retirement" was included for some cases.

Second, the rates for *active participants* were calculated. These rates used the same numerator as the rates for all CYA cases (all arrests during the follow-up period) but used as the denominator only that street time accumulated by those who were arrested at least once for each type of crime (the participants), through the age of their last arrest. These rates thus provide more focused estimates of average arrest rates over periods of active criminal involvement for offenders charged at least once with various crimes. They will, however, overstimate these rates to some unknown extent. A valid estimate would require including the street time of those offenders who committed various crimes but were never arrested for them. In addition, these rates may be inappropriate for assessing group differences or establishing expected rates of arrests for individual offenders when the offense under consideration tends to be committed only once per offender. This latter point will be discussed in detail when the findings for specific offenses are presented.

The analysis for "active participants", then, narrows the focus, eliminating both the bulk of the non-offenders and the post-active street time. As such, it allows for an assessment of the effect of these factors on observed differences in estimated arrest rates among ethnic groups.

Rates for General Categories of Offenses

The aggregate arrest rates (per person-year of street time) for the general categories of offenses are displayed in Table 4.1. Shown are the rates for all cases in the sample and for participants in that offense category. The rates for participants, again, were calculated using only that portion of each offender's street time that occurred prior to the last known arrest.

Over the follow-up period, the rate of arrest overall was one and a half arrests per year of street time for the whole sample. The rate for violent crimes was considerably lower (one arrest for every four to five years of accumulated street time), and charges for property crimes occurred at the rate of one for every three to four years of street time. the lowest rates were found for violent-economic crimes, which occurred at the rate of less than one for every *ten* years of street time. Racial differences followed a similar pattern as for participation, with blacks showing higher overall rates of arrest for each of the crime-types considered, and whites showing the lowest aggregate rates. The ratio of black rates to white rates for violent crimes was over 2:1, with the ratio for violent-economic crimes about 3:1.

When the focus was narrowed to rates for *active participants* in each category of crime, the rates were much higher, as one would expect on the basis

TABLE 4.1 Aggregate yearly arrest rates for offense categories by race.

Offense type	White ($n = 713$)	Black ($n = 359$)	Hispanic ($n = 210$)	Total ($n = 1282$)
All Cases				
Total	1.315[a]	1.847	1.620	1.505
Total violent	.154	.382	.246	.229
Violent-aggressive	.095	.199	.165	.134
Violent-economic	.060	.183	.082	.095
Property	.266	.421	.291	.311
Active Participants				
Total	2.225[b] (682)[c]	2.765 (345)	2.384 (205)	2.404 (1232)
Total violent	.391 (434)	.672 (291)	.447 (167)	.491 (892)
Violent-aggressive	.291 (349)	.420 (231)	.337 (146)	.341 (726)
Violent-economic	.295 (241)	.434 (226)	.264 (97)	.344 (564)
Property	.579 (514)	.735 (295)	.551 (154)	.620 (963)

[a] Number of arrests per person-year of street time.
[b] Number of arrests per person-year of street time through age of last arrest.
[c] Number of cases participating in each category offense.

of removing nonparticipants and some of the street time from the calculations. For all ethnic groups combined, these rates were at least twice as high as those estimated for the entire sample (using all available street time in the estimate). For participants, there were, on average, 2.4 arrest charges for every year of active street time. Participants in violent crimes accumulated one arrest charge for every two years of active street time, and property crime participants were arrested for nearly two property crimes for every three years of accumulated street time. Arrests for violent-aggressive and violent-economic crimes each occurred at a rate of about one for every three years of street time.

Restricting the focus to active participants had the effect of reducing observed differences in these rates across ethnic groups. As a result, the differences in these rates are smaller than those found for the estimates based on all cases and all street time. Although the general pattern of differences among the ethnic groups remained, the rate of violent-economic crimes and property crimes for Hispanic participants fell below those for white participants.

To more easily understand the effect of the narrowed focus on differences in estimated rates among the ethnic groups, the ratios of black and Hispanic rates to those for whites for the two kinds of analysis were calculated. These ratios, with white rates set to one, are shown in Table 4.2. As evidenced from these figures, the ratio of rates decreased when nonparticipants and nonactive periods were removed from the analysis. The ratios of Hispanic rates to white rates, which were not large to begin with, fell to nearly 1:1, with Hispanic rates for violent-aggressive crimes remaining slightly higher and the rates for

TABLE 4.2 Ratios of arrest rates to rates for whites by race.

Offense type	All cases		Active participants	
	Black	Hispanic	Black	Hispanic
Total	1.40	1.23	1.24	1.07
Total violent	2.48	1.60	1.72	1.14
Violent-aggressive	2.09	1.74	1.44	1.16
Violent-economic	3.05	1.37	1.47	.89
Property	1.58	1.09	1.27	.95

violent-economic crimes and property crimes being slightly lower than those for white participants. All of the black rates remained higher than the rates for whites, but the difference was considerably smaller for the more narrowly focused analysis. Thus, while narrowing the focus in this manner eliminated overall differences in rates for Hispanics and whites, it did not eliminate those differences in rates between blacks and whites.

Rates for Specific Crimes

Before presenting the findings, a word of caution is in order with regard to using estimates of *offense-specific* rates of arrest to assess group differences or to establish expected individual rates of arrest. In the previous chapter, multiple arrests for many of the more serious offenses were found to be rare (homicide, rape, and other person offenses, as examples). In calculating the rates of arrest for such crimes, the numerator would be the number of individuals arrested (plus the few additional arrests accumulated by repeaters) and the denominator would be the street time accumulated by the whole sample. For these low-repetition offenses, however, estimated rates will be unreliable because they will, in general, be highly sensitive to the amount of street time available for estimating the rate. For example, if a hypothetical crime is committed only once per offender, that offender's estimated rate of committing that crime would be one divided by the number of street years accumulated during the time he was observed: the longer the observation period, the lower the estimated rate. Thus, for the low-repetition, serious crimes, any estimated rate may be more greatly influenced by the research design (the amount of follow-up available) than by the behavior of the offenders. It is not surprising, in this regard, to find that the estimated "rates" for specific offenses among active offenders reported by Blumstein and Cohen (1979) and Cohen (1986) were around one for every five to seven years, since that was the length of their observation period.

The usefulness of offense-specific arrest rates for establishing expected rates of arrest for *individuals* is even more limited. Some researchers have argued that individual offense rates for offenders who participate in various crimes can be meaningfully estimated from such aggregate, offense-specific rates of arrest (Blumstein and Cohen, 1979; Cohen 1986). In addition to unreliability of these rates at the aggregate level, however, the meaning of a "rate" is often unclear in itself, especially for low-repetition crimes. Offense rates at the individual level connote repetitive commission of the crime in question, with this assumption being more-or-less reasonable for different kinds of crimes. Certainly, a "rate" based on such calculations should not be interpreted as suggesting that other offenders are likely to be arrested at that rate or that the offenders who did commit those crimes would be arrested again if followed long enough. For this reason, findings regarding offense-specific arrest rates should not be interpreted in terms of their indicativeness of the offense rates of *individuals* in the analysis.

The rates of arrest for specific crimes are shown in Table 4.3 for the entire follow-up period for all cases and in Table 4.4 for *active participants*. For the entire sample (all adult street time), the highest rates (ignoring the residual, "other offenses" category) were found for drug-use offenses, which occurred at the rate of one every five years. The only other rate that was higher than one every 10 years of street time was for burglary. These low overall rates are not

TABLE 4.3 Aggregate yearly arrest rate for all cases by offense type by race.

Offense type	White ($n = 713$)	Black ($n = 359$)	Hispanic ($n = 210$)	Total ($n = 1282$)
Homicide	.006	.011	.011	.008
Agg. assault	.054	.130	.100	.082
Rape	.007	.014	.007	.009
Misd. assault	.029	.044	.047	.036
Armed robberty	.025	.066	.034	.037
Strongarm robbery	.023	.094	.038	.044
Other person	.012	.024	.010	.014
Burglary	.117	.191	.157	.143
RSP	.055	.090	.057	.064
Grand theft	.024	.048	.031	.031
Forgery	.049	.052	.022	.045
Grand theft auto	.022	.040	.025	.027
Arson	.002	.003	.002	.003
Other theft	.058	.090	.077	.070
Joyride	.042	.058	.022	.043
Weapons offenses	.053	.103	.050	.066
Sex offenses	.018	.043	.014	.024
Liquor offenses	.085	.069	.156	.093
Drug use	.177	.201	.278	.201
Drug sales	.014	.017	.024	.016
Other offenses	.445	.459	.460	.451

TABLE 4.4 Aggregate yearly arrest rate for active adult period: Cases participating in each offense type[a]

Offense type	White	Black	Hispanic	Total
Homicide	.173	.226	.146	.180
Agg. assault*	.223	.326	.271	.268
Rape	.251	.191	.140	.202
Misd. assault	.179	.202	.184	.187
Armed robbery	.248	.341	.223	.278
Strongarm robberty	.204	.288	.186	.239
Other person	.181	.190	.150	.180
Burglary*	.352	.412	.354	.371
RSP*	.255	.272	.262	.262
Grand theft	.183	.202	.177	.189
Forgery*	.343	.282	.234	.311
Grand theft auto	.191	.221	.191	.202
Arson	.158	.143	.189	.157
Other theft*	.234	.301	.243	.255
Joyride	.262	.259	.172	.250
Weapons offenses*	.267	.305	.229	.275
Sex offenses	.232	.373	.234	.282
Liquor offenses*	.301	.284	.335	.307
Drug use*	.494	.439	.557	.491
Drug sales	.183	.205	.180	.188
Other offenses*	.825	.759	.736	.790

[a] The number of cases included in each estimate can be found in Table 3.2.
*Offenses for which at least 33% of participating offenders had three or more charges (repetitive crimes).

surprising, considering the generally low participation rates for specific offenses. Blacks generally had the highest aggregate arrest rates for all except drug-use offenses and alcohol-related (liquor) offenses; whites generally had the lowest rates, except for joyride (nonfelony auto theft), weapons offenses, and sex offenses. Again, these rates are best thought of as reflecting *group*, rather than *individual* rates of arrest. For example, for each 1000 person-years of street time accumulated by each group (say, 250 individuals contributing four street years each), the blacks, *as a group*, accumulated 130 arrests for aggravated assault, compared to 54 for whites and 100 for Hispanics. The differences among groups can be used to understand factors that influence arrest rates, but they say little about the offense behavior of particular individuals in those groups.

The figures in Table 4.4 indicate that all the rates increased, as expected, when nonparticipants and nonactive street time were excluded. The greatest effect on these rates, of course, resulted from excluding nonparticipants, since the participation rates were generally low. Still, these rates are not very high, reaching a rate of one for every three years of street time only for drug use, burglary, and other offenses.[3]

Once again, the meaning of these rates is not entirely clear, since they are strongly affected by the extent of repetition and the amount of follow-up. For example, a rate of .180 for homicide means that of those ever arrested as adults for homicide offenses, there were 18 arrests for homicide for every 100 years of accumulated street time. Since there were so few cases arrested more than once for homicide, an alternative interpretation is that each 18 offenders arrested for homicide accumulated about 100 person-years of street time during the follow-up period. As indicators of the expected rate of offending, these rates are more indicative of offense behavior for offenses with relatively high repetition rates. In the table, those offenses for which over one-third of the offenders had three or more arrests are shown with an asterisk (*). Of all the rates in the table, the rates for these offenses are the best indicators of arrest rates for individual participants in those offenses. Thus, it might be expected that burglars would be arrested for burglary an average of once every three years, aggravated assaulters an average of once every four years, and so on. It would be less likely that armed robbers would be arrested that often, even though the "rate" for this offense was over .25, since few of the robbers were arrested more than once.

For the high repetition offenses, blacks had the highest rates of arrest for aggravated assault, burglary, receiving stolen property (RSP), theft other than grand theft and weapons offenses. Hispanics had the highest rates of arrest for drug use and liquor offenses, while whites had the highest rates for forgery and for other (miscellaneous) offenses. Although these differences are not large (the greatest difference is for aggravated assault, where the black rate is 1.46 times the rate for whites), they suggest that ethnic differences remain even after controlling to some extent for participation and length of criminal career.

Summary

In general, these analyses have shown that overall rates of arrest were generally high (over 1.5 per year of street time overall and 2.4 per year of active street time for participants). The rates for categories of serious crimes were considerably lower, but, given the seriousness of the offenses, cannot be considered low by any means. Rates for participants during active periods

---

[3] Considering that the present sample constituted a particularly high-risk group of offenders, these rates are remarkably similar to (although somewhat higher than) those provided by Cohen (1986, Table B-19, p. 329) for all adult arrestees in Washington, D.C.:

Aggravated Assault	.19
Robbery	.23
Burglary	.26
Auto Theft	.14
Weapons	.22
Drugs	.32

were nearly two for every three years of street time for property offenses and one every two years for violent offenses. Given that the participation rates for these categories of crime were shown in the previous chapter to be quite high (75% for property crimes and 70% for violent crimes), the overall criminality of this sample of youthful offenders becomes even more apparent. As a group, the offenders who embark on serious criminal careers early in life must be considered likely to be responsible for a substantial amount of crime as adults, and those who do continue their criminal careers into adulthood (and most do) are likely to commit those crimes in which they are involved at substantial rates.

These analyses also showed these aggregate rates to differ by ethnicity. The blacks in the sample, as a group, had higher rates of arrest for each of the general categories of crime, both overall and among active participants. As discussed in the previous chapter, these members of the sample also showed higher levels of participation and higher rates of multiple offending, both within categories and across categories of offenses. Given that ethnicity serves as an indicator of a host of sociocultural differences among the groups, it would appear that social factors influence not only *whether* an individual will engage in various types of criminal behavior, but also the *rate* at which those crimes are committed. A conception of criminal careers that minimizes the importance of these factors by assuming that rates of criminal behavior are, for the most part, immune to social influences (and thereby stable) greatly oversimplifies the nature of those careers.

Arrest Rates by Age: General Offense Categories

These analyses focused on ages 20 to 33 for the cohort of CYA cases, who started their criminal careers early and were followed into adulthood regardless of the nature of their adult criminality. The requirement that supplementary cases have arrests for serious crimes during adulthood (at least one arrest of particular kinds during the follow-up period for probation cases, and adult prison terms for CDC cases) made them less appropriate for studying these effects. Using all cases who were criminally active through at least age 20 (had one or more arrests during or after age 21), total and violent arrest rates were calculated for each age using all available street time for all offenders at that age. Next, to make the findings more comparable to those obtained in the pivotal study of arrest rates by age undertaken by Blumstein and Cohen (1979), the analysis was restricted to cases who were active in crime at each age: those offenders who had arrests after each age in question.[4] To

---

[4] Rates for ages prior to age 20 and after age 33 were not analyzed, because some individuals were selected for CYA on the basis of crimes occurring during ages 18 and 19 and there were too few cases active at ages beyond 34 for analysis. In some analyses, rates for ages 18 to 19 were used as control variables, to determine the effect of prior criminality on patterns of change.

avoid spuriously inflating the estimates of rates for later ages, data for the year during which the last arrest occurred were not used in the analyses for active offenders.

Rates for All Cases with Follow-up Data

To set the stage for understanding the effects of limiting the analysis to periods of active criminal involvement, patterns over the entire follow-up period were calculated for all cases included in the analysis of active periods (all cases who were active beyond age 20). Assuming the absence of any systematic change by age in the probability of being arrested for crimes, changes at this level will reflect the effects both of any reduction in the number of cohort members remaining active in crime and of any reduction in the rate at which active criminals commit their crimes. These rates, along with the percent of all arrests that were for violent offenses, are shown in Table 4.5. These figures indicate that over the 14-year period, total arrest rates for this cohort decreased from 2.81 arrests per person-year of street time at age 18 to .54 arrests at age 33. The violent arrest rate showed a similar, though not as steep, overall decline with age. Note that the slower decline for violent arrests resulted in a slight increase in the percentage of violent arrests for later ages.

Table 4.6 and the accompanying graphs (Figures 4.1 and 4.2) show the arrest rates for the same cases during periods of active involvement in crime. These rates exhibit a similar overall decrease over time, with total rates dropping from 2.81 to 1.08 (a drop of over 60%) and violent rates dropping from .36 to .17 (a drop of over 50%). It appears that the decreases in arrest by age shown

TABLE 4.5 Arrest rates by age.

Age	N^a	Total rate	Violent rate	Violent percent
20	1180	2.81	.36	12.8%
21	1180	2.68	.33	12.4%
22	1180	2.40	.37	15.3%
23	1180	2.10	.32	15.1%
24	1180	1.83	.28	15.3%
25	1172	1.55	.28	18.1%
26	1150	1.37	.23	16.6%
27	1099	1.23	.27	21.6%
28	1041	1.08	.20	18.5%
29	981	.97	.16	16.6%
30	901	.83	.14	17.1%
31	803	.82	.18	21.5%
32	687	.55	.13	22.7%
33	593	.54	.10	17.9%

[a] Rate calculations for each age include all cases with follow-up data through that age.

TABLE 4.6 Arrest rates by age for active offenders.

Age	N^a	Total rate	Violent rate	Violent percent
20	1180	2.81	.36	12.8%
21	1152	2.65	.33	12.3%
22	1107	2.42	.35	14.4%
23	1041	2.18	.31	14.4%
24	961	1.98	.28	14.3%
25	866	1.78	.29	16.5%
26	756	1.57	.21	13.5%
27	537	1.48	.30	20.2%
28	524	1.41	.22	15.4%
29	405	1.42	.16	11.6%
30	328	1.56	.28	18.2%
31	254	1.51	.25	16.5%
32	204	1.08	.21	19.4%
33	142	1.08	.17	16.0%

[a] Rate calculations for each age include only those offenders who had both follow-up data through the next higher age and at least one arrest after the present age.

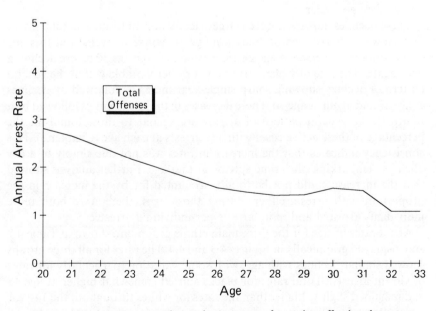

FIGURE 4.1 Aggregate yearly total arrest rates for active offenders by age.

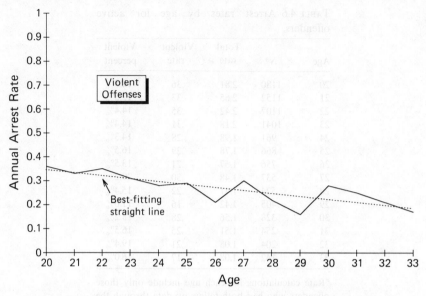

FIGURE 4.2 Aggregate yearly violent arrest rates for active offenders by age.

for all cases with follow-up is not simply caused by more and more cases dropping out of crime altogether. Not only did some cases desist completely, the remaining, active cases tended to commit crimes at an increasingly lower rate as they got older.

These declines, however, were neither steady nor uniform. The total arrest rate showed a fairly even decline until age 26, where it leveled out to some extent and then reversed at age 28, increasing through age 30 before declining once again. The rate of violent arrests was rather variable within the general pattern of decline, showing sharp single-year increases followed by declines at age 27 and again at age 30. These increases in the late twenties followed by a return to the general pattern of decline are similar to those found for the percentage of these active cases with any arrests at each age (Chapter 3). This consistency indicates that the increase in rates was not due simply to a few offenders embarking on "crime sprees" at that age. Further analysis showed that the increase could not be totally accounted for by the increase in the proportion with arrests either; during those ages, there were both more individuals arrested and more arrests per individual arrestee.

Arrest rates by age for the three main ethnic groups are shown in Table 4.7 and displayed graphically in Figures 4.3 and 4.4. The rates for all three groups showed similar declines with age, with some variation (particularly for rates of violent arrests). Total rates for blacks started somewhat higher at age 18 and remained slightly higher than the rates for whites throughout the 14-year range. Rates for Hispanics varied between those for whites and blacks. All

TABLE 4.7 Arrest rates by age for active offenders by race

Age		N^a	Total rate	Violent rate	Violent percent
Whites:	20	654	2.66	.23	8.7%
	21	634	2.40	.22	9.2%
	22	610	2.23	.25	11.0%
	23	565	2.00	.24	12.2%
	24	516	1.81	.24	13.0%
	25	457	1.50	.16	11.0%
	26	393	1.33	.14	10.5%
	27	328	1.17	.19	16.0%
	28	269	1.18	.21	18.0%
	29	202	1.39	.13	9.3%
	30	157	1.36	.18	13.5%
	31	114	1.53	.20	12.9%
	32	95	.96	.17	17.7%
	33	67	.92	.11	11.5%
Blacks:	20	330	3.28	.68	20.7%
	21	325	3.34	.58	17.3%
	22	310	2.74	.61	22.3%
	23	298	2.39	.46	19.5%
	24	277	2.29	.38	16.4%
	25	251	2.26	.59	26.2%
	26	227	1.85	.35	19.0%
	27	195	1.94	.50	25.7%
	28	158	1.71	.22	12.7%
	29	122	1.58	.20	12.8%
	30	102	1.89	.37	19.4%
	31	80	1.54	.24	15.7%
	32	64	1.19	.32	26.7%
	33	45	1.29	.18	14.3%
Hispanics:	20	196	2.59	.31	11.9%
	21	193	2.43	.30	12.3%
	22	187	2.56	.31	12.2%
	23	178	2.44	.31	12.7%
	24	168	2.08	.30	14.5%
	25	158	1.93	.25	13.2%
	26	136	1.82	.20	11.0%
	27	114	1.61	.29	17.7%
	28	97	1.59	.23	14.6%
	29	81	1.24	.19	15.5%
	30	69	1.52	.39	25.6%
	31	60	1.45	.36	25.0%
	32	45	1.20	.15	12.2%
	33	30	1.11	.32	29.2%

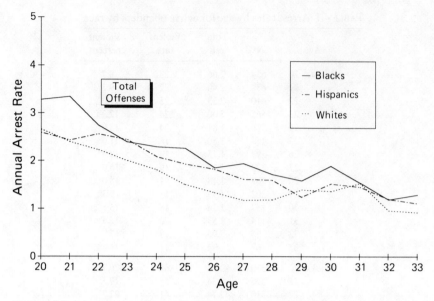

FIGURE 4.3 Aggregate yearly total arrest rates for active offenders by age by race.

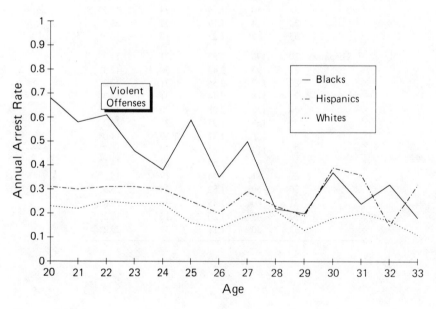

FIGURE 4.4 Aggregate yearly violent arrest rates for active offenders by age by race.

three rates showed similar increases around age 30, indicating the pervasiveness of this somewhat anomalous pattern. Rates of violent arrests, too, showed similar patterns of increase at around age 27 and again around age 30 for all groups (blacks had one additional peak at age 25). In fact, for Hispanics, the highest rates of arrest for violent crimes occurred during the early thirties.

In order to assess the influence of early adult rates on later rates of arrest, rates by age (for total arrests) were also calculated for offenders classified as high-, medium-, or low-rate based on arrests occurring during ages 18 and 19 (Figure 4.5). Three particularly noteworthy patterns emerged from this analysis. First, the total arrest rates during these early adult years carried over into the remainder of the twenties. While all the rates declined during this period, the relative ranking of the groups in terms of their rates of arrest was maintained. Second, there appeared to be a lower limit to the arrest rates for these active offenders of around one arrest per year. The rates for the three groups tended to converge on this lower limit at around age 32 to 33. Third, all three groups showed the previously mentioned rise in rates during the late twenties, with the rise coming slightly earlier for low-rate offenders and slightly later (and most noticeably) for medium-rate offenders. Thus, while differences in aggregate rates of criminal behavior during the early adult period were maintained through the twenties, all three groups experienced some decline in those rates, and the rate of decline was faster for those offenders who were the most active while younger.

Rates of arrest for violent offenses for these three groups showed a similar pattern: higher rates for those with the highest early-adult rates and a general

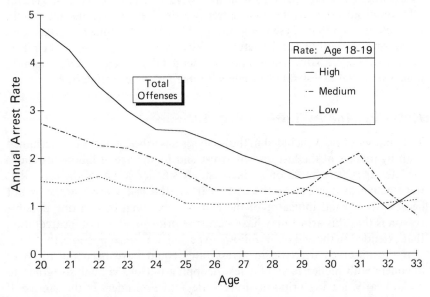

FIGURE 4.5 Aggregate yearly total arrest rates for active offenders by age by arrest rate during ages 18 to 19.

convergence over time. Further, the proportion of arrests that were for violent offenses showed no particular pattern, suggesting that the decline in rates for the high-rate early-adult group was not simply a matter of their reducing their minor criminal activity while maintaining higher levels of serious criminal activity.

In addition to the analysis described so far, others were performed to help understand these findings and to assess their applicability to particular types of offenders. The results are summarized in the following sections.

Rates by Age by Year of Birth

To differentiate between *age effects, cohort effects* (effects resulting from common experiences shared by various birth cohorts), and *period effects* (effects resulting from experiences shared in common throughout the sample at a particular point in time—and therefore at different ages for different cohorts), it is best to estimate rates by age for various birth cohorts followed through time. Unfortunately, the sample of CYA cases was primarily drawn from two previous research studies occurring five years apart at two different institutions. Because these institutions were used to house delinquents differing in seriousness (the more serious, older delinquents in the earlier study), birth cohorts necessarily differed in the extent of their delinquency. No attempt was made, therefore, to differentiate age, period, and cohort effects for this sample.

However, aggregate rates by age were estimated for three birth cohorts to assess whether similar patterns of decline were noted in each case. In general, all three groups showed the same patterns of decline with age and showed the characteristic jump in these rates during ages 29 to 31. While there was some variation across groups in the actual rates estimated for ages and in the rate of decline with age, no discernible pattern emerged that would cast doubt on the conclusion that arrest rates decline with age for these offenders.

Rates by Age by Last Active Age

The number of cases included in the analyses described so far was determined both by the age at the last known arrest and by the age at follow-up. Rates for later ages were based on an increasingly smaller subset of the cases that were active at age 21. As discussed earlier, the last known arrest is not necessarily a valid indicator of the end of a criminal career; one possible reason is that this arrest may have occurred prior to a term of incarceration that extended to the end of the follow-up period. It seemed possible, therefore, that the observed decrease in arrest rates could have been the result of offenders with higher rates of arrest dropping out of the analysis (going to prison) early, leaving primarily lower-rate active offenders in the sample. If this were the case, the overall decline would have been observed in spite of stable rates across offenders who were "active" up to various ages. To test this possibility, rates by age (and for the entire active follow-up period) were calculated separately for groups whose last active age was the same. While there was considerable variation in these rates by age within groups, each group showed a general decline with age and no substantial variation was found in overall rates for the different groups. The results of these analyses indicated that the observed declines by age could not be explained simply on the basis of which cases were in the analysis at each age.

Rates for Particular Offenders

Analysis of rates by age were also performed separately for CYA cases who went to prison as adults and, within subsample, robbers and burglars. The latter analyses were performed because these offenders have been considered by some to be among the most active and persistent offenders (Greenwood, 1982). Similar declines were found in all analyses. The rates for all cases going to adult prison ($n = 485$) stated at a relatively high rate (4.51) and declined fairly steadily to 1.58 at age 33. There was a small, but noticeable rise in the rate at age 30, with a decline thereafter. Violent arrest rates for this sample also started relatively high (.75) and declined to .24 at age 33, with the same small jump at age 30.

These general observations hold also for robbers ($n = 218$) and burglars ($n = 189$) in this prison sample. Both groups showed a slightly lower rate of decline (from just over 4.0 per street year to around 2.0 per street year over that period) than did the prison sample as a whole. There were considerable differences between these two subgroups in terms of rates of violent arrests, however. Robbers had much higher rates of violent arrests at age 20 (1.24, compared to .51 for burglars), but showed a much sharper decline, falling below burglars in the rate of these arrests at age 33 (.20 vs. .32). Consequently, the burglars showed an overall increase in the percentage of arrests that were violent, while robbers showed a decrease. Both groups had small increases in these rates around age 30.

Arrest Rates by Age: Specific Offenses

The analyses of arrest rates for specific offenses were carried out somewhat differently from those for all offenses and all violent offenses. In most cases, there were relatively few offenders involved and fewer yet who had more than one or two arrests. Consequently, it seemed likely that there would be only, at most, a handful of arrests occurring at each age; under these conditions, a difference of one or two arrests from one age to the next could result in wide variations in estimated rates. Rather than obtain rates for each specific age, estimates were calculated for four-year age blocks (18–21, 22–25, 26–29, 30–33, 34–37). This kind of aggregation was intended to smooth out some of the random variation while still maintaining enough points to allow an assessment of trends over time. Analyses focused on arrest rates for specific offenses for all active offenders, rates for serious offenses for active offenders who participated in these crimes at some point during their adult follow-up, and the subsequent rates (during active periods) for offenders involved in robbery or burglary offenses during the 18–21 age bracket.

Each of these analyses was designed to investigate trends in arrest rates for specific offenses over time in a slightly different way. Analyses involving all active offenders provided a basis for understanding the expected offense behavior of the cohort as a whole as it aged into the early thirties. The inclusion of nonparticipants in the rates, however, may have masked some variation in the rate at which these crimes were committed by participants, prompting the analysis of these rates for participants only. Since once again, these offenses often result in only one or two arrests per individual, even the rates for participants may not provide a clear picture of rates over time. These rates may be more indicative of *when* offenders of particular types finally commit those offenses than of their relative *rates* of committing those offenses at different ages. The final analyses focused on offenders known to have been arrested for particular crimes early in their adult careers. Their rates of arrest at later ages provide another picture of how offense behavior changes as a function of age for particular offenders.

Note that these analyses were performed on a data set created especially for this purpose, and that this data set differed slightly from that used in the previous analyses. Specifically, because of some miscoding of final follow-up dates in the file used in the earlier analyses, some later offenses were lost, resulting in a smaller number of known "active" offenders at various ages. These errors were basically arbitrary (and random) and could not have affected the general findings in any important way. Nevertheless, the number of offenders included in the following analyses is slightly higher at each age than in the previous analyses.

Specific Arrest Rates for All Active Offenders

Shown in Table 4.8 are the arrest rates for categories of offenses, the average number of different types of crimes (among the 21 types listed) for which these offenders were arrested and the rates for specific offenses for cases active through each age block. The rates for total offenses and all violent offenses are included on this table to allow comparison with the rates by age presented in Table 4.6. These rate estimates are consistent, suggesting that the present analysis is sufficiently sensitive to changes in rates over time to serve our purposes. However, by aggregating across ages 30 to 33, some information was lost. The "jump" in rates (noted earlier) that occurred around age 30 affected this entire block of ages. Consequently, interpretation of changes for this last block must be somewhat tentative.

Arrest rates for the general categories of offenses over the first three blocks showed the same general decline in rates as was found in the previous analyses.

TABLE 4.8 Aggregate yearly arrest rates for age blocks: Active offenders

	Age			
Offense type	18–21 ($n = 1159$)	22–25 ($n = 921$)	26–29 ($n = 505$)	30–33 ($n = 181$)
Total	3.011	2.113	1.551	1.439
Violent-aggressive	.202	.198	.153	.143
Violent-economic	.169	.125	.094	.120
Property	.597	.435	.334	.425
Total violent	.371	.321	.247	.263
Average no. of types	3.780	3.096	2.634	2.464
Violent-aggressive				
Homicide	.008	.009	.003	.007
Agg. assault	.125	.121	.098	.081
Rape	.015	.011	.007	.010
Misd. assault	.055	.056	.046	.045
Violent-economic				
Armed robbery	.058	.053	.034	.031
Strongarm robbery	.092	.052	.042	.064
Other person	.018	.020	.018	.026
Property				
Burglary	.298	.211	.150	.139
Rec. stolen property	.102	.099	.072	.091
Grand theft	.048	.041	.043	.043
Forgery	.074	.055	.039	.136
Grand theft auto	.076	.029	.030	.015
Other				
Arson	.006	.002	.001	.002
Other theft	.124	.100	.078	.093
Joyride	.120	.046	.022	.022
Weapons offenses	.089	.090	.084	.072
Sex offenses	.041	.027	.029	.028
Liquor offenses	.189	.172	.103	.050
Drug use	.378	.303	.235	.162
Drug sales	.023	.026	.021	.026
Other offenses	1.072	.591	.396	.296

The average number of types per offender also declined over these ages, suggesting that for this cohort, the effect of age on criminal behavior involved both a decrease in the overall number of crimes committed *and* in the overall breadth of criminal involvement. However, property and violent-economic arrest rates showed an increase for this last block; whether these increases actually signal a sustained rise in these arrest rates after age 30 cannot be determined from these data.

The rates for specific offenses in Table 4.8 indicate that for these active offenders, the arrest rates for most of the specific crimes generally declined over time, at least through the first three blocks. Exceptions included homicide and other person offenses (both of which are low-rate, nonrepetitive crimes), along with grand theft, weapons offenses, sex offenses, and drug sales. The rate of arrests for strongarm robbery, receiving stolen property (RSP), forgery, and other theft showed a rise in the 30 to 33 age bracket, after exhibiting decreases up to that point. Again, whether these rates experienced momentary rises around age 30 or continued to rise throughout the early thirties could not be determined with these data.

Specific Rates for Active Participants

Table 4.9 shows the effect of limiting the calcuation of arrest rates over active periods to those offenders who participated in the various crimes. In general, while all the rates were higher, the same overall patterns remained. Except for homicide and other person offenses, for which the rates were highest during the 22 to 25 age block, all these offenses showed decreases in rates over the twenties. On the other hand, all these rates showed an increase after age 30, with the exceptions of aggravated assault, armed robbery, burglary, and

TABLE 4.9 Aggregate yearly arrest rates for age blocks: Active offenders participating in each offense type

		Age				
Offense type	N^a	18–21	22–25	26–29	30–33	Total
Violent-aggressive						
Homicide	89	.116	.163	.047	.108	.115
Agg. assault	550	.274	.247	.190	.148	.237
Rape	85	.224	.169	.100	.138	.173
Misd. assault	323	.194	.178	.135	.140	.171
Violent-economic						
Armed robbery	295	.276	.272	.161	.136	.241
Strongarm robbery	357	.329	.183	.127	.161	.223
Other person	153	.148	.156	.141	.152	.149
Property						
Burglary	726	.503	.337	.225	.194	.364
Rec. stolen property	456	.272	.251	.179	.240	.243
Grand theft	302	.193	.157	.151	.159	.169
Forgery	253	.337	.233	.131	.577	.280
Grand theft auto	238	.393	.144	.108	.047	.220

[a] The number of cases participating in these crimes as adults who also had both follow-up time and offenses of some kind after age 21. The number of cases in each later cell is that subset of these cases that had both follow-up and one or more offenses in the next later block.

TABLE 4.10 Aggregate yearly arrest rates for age blocks: Active burglars and robbers at age 18–21

	Age			
Offense type	18–21	22–25	26–29	30–33
Burglars (n = 497)				
Total	4.216	2.424	1.836	1.534
Violent	.458	.374	.342	.259
Burglary	.743	.287	.187	.148
Robbers (n = 293)				
Total	4.533	2.605	2.113	1.738
Violent	1.084	.523	.405	.452
Robbery	.703	.228	.142	.195

grand theft auto. Note, however, that none of these rates increased to the level found for either of the first two age blocks.

Subsequent Arrest Rates of Early Offenders

The final analysis focused on the arrest rates, over subsequent age blocks, of those offenders arrested for burglary or robbery[5] during the 18 to 21 age block. Shown in Table 4.10 are the rates during active blocks for all offenses, all violent offenses, and either burglary or robbery. For the 497 burglars in the analysis, all the rates showed a clear decline through all three subsequent blocks, the greatest drop generally occurring for the second age block (from 18–21 to 22–25). The arrest rate for burglary dropped over 80% from the first to the fourth block. For robbers, a similar decline was found for total offenses and, through the first two subsequent blocks, for all violent offenses and for robbery offenses specifically. The violent and robbery rates increased during the last block, but, again, did not reach the level found for the 22 to 25 block. Despite this increase after age 30 (which may not be characteristic of these four ages), the robbery rate during the last block was still only 28% of the rate for the 18 to 21 block.

Summary

These various analyses of arrest rates as a function of age for this cohort of offenders produced surprisingly consistent results: rates of arrest generally decreased throughout the twenties, with some indication of levelling off or slightly increasing during the very early thirties for a number of offenses.

---

[5] Both armed robbery and strongarm robbery were included.

Similar results were obtained for total offenses, violent offenses, and specific crimes, as well as for various subgroups of offenders (participants vs. others, different ethnic groups, offenders going to adult prison, cases with different early rates of arrest, robbers and burglars). Although the declines were not great in all cases, the same pattern generally held. Recalling the earlier findings that overall participation in crimes (the percentage of active offenders arrested at each age) decreased and that the average number of types of crimes decreased as well, the present findings lead to the conclusion that, in general, offense behavior clearly declined with age for these serious offenders even while they remained active in crime.

Chapter 5
Individual Offense Rates: Methodological Issues

So far, the discussion has focused on general patterns of criminal participation and of rates of arrest within a cohort of former serious juvenile offenders. In those analyses, rates were estimated using aggregated data on the number of arrests and the amount of street time during the follow-up period. In the following chapters, attention will turn to issues related to the criminal careers of *individual offenders*: their stability and predictiveness. To address these issues, individual-level data on the rates of arrest over portions of the follow-up period were used. Analyses focused on whether offense behavior tended to remain relatively stable over time and on the feasibility of identifying those offenders with the highest rates of arrest. Before presenting these findings, it is important to first gain an understanding of the limitations of official data for addressing these types of issues.

It is well known that official criminal history data provide, at best, an incomplete picture of an individual's criminal behavior.[1] Arrests can be seen as a "sample" of all the crimes an individual commits, with the sampling probability being a "loose" function of the probabilities of arrest for various crimes. These probabilities may be expected to vary somewhat for individuals (some are better able to avoid detection), over time (a police department may obtain extra funding to "crack down" on certain crimes), and across jurisdictions, but overall it is possible to view arrests as a more-or-less "random" sampling of crimes committed. Now, by the nature of random sampling devices, no two random samples of a given population will be expected to be exactly alike, and no single sample will be expected to perfectly represent that population. Thus, any arrest rate based on an offender's criminal record (over, say, a four-year period) will only approximate the actual rate of criminal behavior during that period, and any *two* of these rates (say,

---

[1] Although there is the problem of "false arrests," which (when the focus is on charged offenses, regardless of conviction) may spuriously inflate the estimate of an individual offender's involvement in crime, the greatest source of error is probably in the other direction: many more actual crimes than arrest records would suggest (Blumstein et al., 1986).

adjacent four-year periods) will provide somewhat different estimates of the individual's criminal behavior *even if that behavior is exactly the same during those two periods.* To the extent that the arrest process is truly random, these deviations from the actual rates can be thought of as resulting from "random measurement error."

This limitation of official offense data has important implications for the analysis of stability and predictability of offense patterns. On the one hand, a less-than-perfect correlation between arrest rates over different periods of time would be expected even for offenders whose actual criminal behavior did not change. On the other hand, given some modicum of ability to predict criminal behavior, that ability would be reduced simply by the fact of using official data. Of importance in both cases is the *extent* of the reduction that would be expected. For studying stability, the issue is how to interpret findings on the relationship between arrest rates observed for different periods for the same individuals: how much these rates would be expected to vary by chance (random measurement error) alone. In other words, what is needed is an estimate of *expected* variation in arrest rates, given no change in criminal behavior, that can be used as a standard for evaluating *actual* variation.

For predictability, the important issue is simply the extent to which the use of official data limits the ability to predict offense behavior. Many possible policies in criminal justice (from focusing efforts at rehabilitation to selective incapacitation) rest on the ability to identify individuals most likely to continue offending at relatively high rates. Since in most cases, only official data are available for making these predictions, an understanding of the limitations of official data can help in evaluating the feasibility of these policies.

The present approach to addressing both these issues involved estimating the relationship of the observed data (arrest rates) for two sample periods during which the underlying variable (criminal behavior) was expected to be identical. Following the suggestion by Janson (1983), each individual sample member's follow-up data were divided into those referring to odd ages (ages 19, 21, 23, etc.) and those referring to even ages. Data for ages 18 to 37 were used, so that there were 10 years of possible data included in each observation period, but since not all cases were followed through that age, the number of years in each observation varies across individuals.

Offense rates for total offenses and violent offenses were calculated for both even and odd ages by adding all arrest charges for those ages and dividing that number by the number of street years the individual accumulated during those ages. Cases with less than one full year of street time during either odd or even ages were eliminated. To reduce the effect of skewness on measures of association, the natural logarithms of these variables were used in the analyses. Similarly, percentages of street time on various types of drugs, percentages of street time employed and percentages of total time in various marital statuses were calculated for both odd and even ages. Although some normal fluctuation in *behavior* may be expected from one year to the next, it was expected that these fluctuations would average out, leaving differences in observed rates between odd and even ages to indicate primarily the amount of variation resulting from measurement error.

Split-half Correlations

Correlations between the odd- and even-age variables (which will be referred to as "split-half correlations"), along with Spearman-Brown reliability coefficients and r-squared values, are shown in Table 5.1. The correlations of the logged offense-rate variables were not very high, considering that the underlying variable (actual criminal behavior) should be very highly correlated. The correlation for the violent offense rate was especially low, indicating that over the follow-up period, the rate of violent arrests for any sampling period was unlikely to be highly correlated with the rate for any other period, even if the underlying behavior was reasonably stable. The correlation for total arrests was not as low, and may seem reasonably high when compared to other behavioral indices, but still suggests some profound limitations on the usefulness of official data for predictive purposes. The proportion of explained variance for the total offense rate was only .53, meaning that the total arrest rate over as much as 10 years accounted for only 53% of the variance in an equivalent 10-year period for these offenders.

As an index of the relative seriousness of the offenses committed by each individual, the percentage of all arrests that were for violent offenses was also calculated. This correlation, labeled "percent violent" was even lower, apparently affected by measurement error in both of the other variables. Thus, under the best of conditions (known stability of offense behavior), the

TABLE 5.1 Split-half correlations and reliabilities.

Variable	N	Pearson correlation $[r]$	Reliability coefficients $[2r/(1 + r)]$	Explained variance $[r^2]$
Arrest Rate (Logged)				
Total	. 1538	.727	.842	.529
Violent	1538	.448	.618	.201
Percent violent	1538	.259	.411	.067
Percent of Street Time				
Heroin use	924	.881	.937	.776
Speed/barbiturates use	924	.869	.930	.755
Hallucinogens use	924	.863	.927	.745
Full-time employment	924	.801	.641	.641
Unemployed	924	.822	.676	.676
Percent of All Follow-up				
Common-law relationship	964	.958	.918	.918
Legally married	964	.971	.943	.943
Supporting dependents	964	.972	.944	.944

ability to predict using a considerable amount of official data on criminal behavior would appear to be severely limited, especially for violent offenses.

Also shown in the table are the split-half correlations for measures of drug use, employment, and marital status. Recall that due to the rather fragmentary nature of the file materials from which these data were coded, it was necessary to make assumptions about the stability of these factors. For drug use and marital status, it was assumed that indicated statuses continued unchanged until actual evidence of a change was noted in the file (only known changes in drug-use patterns and marital status were coded). The coding for these variables may well have "built in" some amount of stability that was not true of these variables. It is not surprising, therefore, that these variables correlated almost perfectly. Still there was considerable evidence of change in these patterns (few had the same pattern through the entire follow-up period), especially for drug use. Consequently, drug-use correlations are somewhat lower than those for marital status.

Employment was coded as the approximate number of months worked during calendar years (since that was how employment was generally indicated in the files) and whether that employment was primarily full-time or part-time. Being unable to work during a given year (being disabled or in school) was coded as well, leaving the absence of any data to indicate unemployment for that year. Thus, for these variables, errors are probably quite random, though considerable. For example, a notation that a particular individual "worked full-time for five months in 1982" was coded just that way, even though the actual employment may have spanned calendar years to some extent. This kind of imprecision is reflected in the relatively low split-half correlations for these variables.

In an attempt to isolate the factors that may have caused the low offense-rate correlations, they were recalculated after placing certain restrictions on the sample or the data. The results are shown in Table 5.2. First, in order to understand the relationship between the length of the sampling period and the correlations, correlations were obtained using various numbers of the odd-age and even-age years. Care was taken to choose ages so that the average age for the sampled years was the same odd and even. In general, as the number of years used to produce the rate decreased, so did the correlations between the odd and even estimates. Two of these correlations—for eight-year (two estimates) and four-year groups[2] (four estimates)—are shown in the table.

---

[2] The four sets of four-year groups of ages included the following ages:

Set 1 even: 18, 20, 24, 26
       odd: 19, 21, 23, 25

Set 2 even: 20, 22, 24, 26
       odd: 19, 21, 25, 27

Set 3 even: 20, 22, 26, 28
       odd: 19, 23, 25, 29

Set 4 even: 22, 24, 26, 28
       odd: 21, 23, 27, 29

TABLE 5.2 Split-half correlations of arrest rates (logged) under varying data conditions.

Condition	Number of cases	Total rate (Logged)	Violent rate (Logged)
Ages Included			
Eight (avg. of 2 est.)	1538	.704	.415
Four (avg. of 4 est.)	1538	.597	.295
Truncation			
Top 2%	1538	.729	.452
Top 5%	1538	.728	.444
Elimination			
Top 2%	1467	.695	
	1463		.366
Top 5%	1398	.674	
	1409		.334
Minimum No. of Offenses			
Two or more	855		.174
Five or more	1315	.638	
	347		−.015
Ten or more	1036	.568	
Minimum Street Years			
1	1538	.727	.448
2	1454	.722	.437
3	1293	.702	.418
4	1138	.686	.349
5	684	.644	.336

Note that the four-year correlations are only about 60% as high as the ten-year correlations.

To assess the effect of skewness on these correlations, analyses were performed in which the highest rate values were truncated (using the 95th and 98th percentiles as cut-offs) and in which the highest rate cases were simply eliminated altogether. As shown in the table, these efforts resulted in no improvement; in fact, the elimination of the top 5% of cases actually resulted in lower overall correlations.

Basing the analysis on cases with a minimum number of offenses allowed for the determination of whether larger numbers of arrests would be spread more evenly among odd and even ages. The *lower* rates for the more repetitive offenders came as something of a surprise, suggesting that arrest rates are no better indicators of offense behavior for relatively high-rate arrestees than for others.

Finally, the impact of differences in the amount of street time across offenders was assessed by restricting the analysis to cases with varying numbers of street years during both the odd and even ages. Again, the greater the restriction, the lower the correlation. Similar results were found when correlations using rates calculated for four ages were analyzed (not shown). In this case, it appears that the increasing street-year requirement increasingly selected out cases with the highest arrest rates (these offenders apparently spent a great deal of time incarcerated), reducing both the overall base-rate and the amount of variation. Both these effects tend to reduce correlations.

In general, it appears that low probabilities of arrest rather severely reduce the reliability of arrest rates as indicators of offense behavior for individuals. Even using up to 10 years of arrest information odd and even, the correlation for total offense rates was moderate and that for violent offense rates was very low. Correlations based on smaller numbers of years were lower. Thus, the usefulness of offense rates based on what is usually considered a relatively long follow-up period (four years) for differentiating among offenders with different actual offense rates is suspect. Their usefulness for establishing relative rates of violent offenses is particularly problematic. The problem, further, did not appear to be caused by the skewness of the rate variables, the inclusion of low-rate (or non-) offenders in the correlations, or the inclusion of cases with small amounts of street time. The arrest process would simply seem to be inherently limited in its ability to produce a reliable sampling of an individual's offenses.

Of course, it is reasonable that some of the lack of high correlations is due simply to short-term variation in criminal behavior. A momentary "crime spree" after a prolonged period of low-rate offending, for example, may result in a single year's total of offenses being higher than all other years combined. Further, a large number of arrests in a given year is likely to lead to some considerable response by the justice system, placing rather strong limitations on the number of arrests likely to occur during the next year (the offender may be incarcerated or threatened with such if the behavior continues). The same limitation is not as likely for previously low-rate offenders, making *changes* in rates from low to high, or high to low, more likely than remaining high-rate for any length of time. These effects would be expected to be even more pronounced for ordinarily low-rate, relatively serious (i.e., violent) offenses.

Correspondence of Rankings Based on Rates of Arrest

Correlations tell us something about the relationship between the rates of arrest calculated for the odd and even ages, but it is possible that these rates are too "precisely" calculated, so that reasonable correspondence between rates is masked by relatively small, and unimportant, differences in the calculated rates. In other words, cases with relatively high rates of arrest during both odd and even ages may still show considerable variation in actual rates; this variation may produce low correlations even though, for practical purposes, these cases were stably high-rate offenders. Accordingly, offenders were classified as having low, medium, or high rates during odd and even years, and the extent of agreement in these rankings was calculated. The same cut-off points were used for both odd and even ages. For odd and even ages over the whole follow-up period, cut-off points were based on the distribution of rates over the entire career (all ages combined). For the various four-year analyses, cut-off points were chosen for each odd/even pair such that approximately the same number of cases were classified as high, medium, and low. Cross tabulations provided a basis for determining the amount of agreement.

Table 5.3 shows the number of cases in each cell for the cross tabulation of total offense rates over the full follow-up period. Simple calculations show that of the 377 cases identified as low-rate for the even ages, 244 (or 65%) were also low-rate during the odd ages. The corresponding figure for even-to-odd correspondence was $244/418 = 58\%$, for an average of 61.5% agreement overall for the low-rate group. Average correspondence figures for the medium and high-rate groups were 55.6% and 72.1%, respectively. These figures, especially for the high-rate offenders, appear fairly high, suggesting reasonable correspondence between odd and even years. However, the percentage of cases that were identified as high-rate during *either* the odd or even years who were identified as such in *both* odd and even ages, was only $377/(535 + 511 - 377) = 56.4\%$. In other words, only about 56% of the offenders who were identified as high-rate, based on one sample of ages or the other, were high-rate in both sample periods.

For violent offense rate categories (Table 5.4), the above calculations produce lower correspondence estimates, as would be expected from the lower correlations. Average correspondence rates for low, medium, and high-rate offenders were, repsectively, 63.0%, 41.8%, and 49.0%. For the high-rate

TABLE 5.3 Correspondence of odd/even arrest rates: Total offenses.

| | | *Odd* | | | |
		Low	medium	High	Total
	Low	244	120	13	377 (24.5%)
Even	Medium	162	343	121	626 (40.7%)
	High	12	146	377	535 (34.8%)
	Total	418	609	511	1538
		(27.2%)	(39.6%)	(33.2%)	(100%)

TABLE 5.4 Correspondence of odd/even arrest rates: Violent offenses.

| | | *Odd* | | | |
		Low	Medium	High	Total
	Low	449	154	75	678 (44.1%)
Even	Medium	226	203	108	537 (34.9%)
	High	74	85	164	323 (21.0%)
	Total	749	442	347	1538
		(48.7%)	(28.7%)	(22.6%)	(100%)

offenders identified as such for either odd or even ages, only 32.4% were high-rate during both odd cnd even ages. Thus, the usefulness of arrest rates for identifying offenders who had high-rates of arrest in comparable time periods was quite limited for violent offenses.

Since the analysis of offense rate stability over time (Chapter 6) will focus on four-year blocks of ages, the same calculations were performed for the four sets of matching four-year groups of odd and even ages. The average of the eight correspondence rates (even to odd and odd to even for the four cross-tabulations) were

    Low: 61.2%
Medium: 43.4%
    High: 61.0%

Thus, only about 61% of high-rate arrestees identified on the basis of four years of data were also identified as high-rate in a comparable four years of data.

In these analyses for violent arrest rates, it was not possible to trichotomize the rates, since over 60% of offenders in each four-year age group had *no* violent arrests. Analyses were performed, therefore, with the variable dichotomized as "no arrests" versus "any arrests." The variable was split so as to identify the 20% of cases with the highest rates. For the none/any analysis, an average of 73.2% of those with no violent arrests during one set of four ages also had no violent arrests during the corresponding ages (odd or even); conversely, 26.8% of these offenders with no offenses over four years *did* have a violent arrest in the comparable period. Of the cases that did have violent arrests, an average of only 51.4% also had arrests during the comparable four years (almost half of the violent offenders were not identified as such using data from a comparable period). The average correspondence rates for identified high-rate violent offenders (the top 20%) was 37.9%; in contrast, an average of 42.5% of these relatively high-rate violent offenders had *no* violent arrests during the comparable four ages. Clearly, the usefulness of data on rates of violent arrests for identifying offenders with a potential for violence does not appear to be very great. Only about four in every 10 offenders with high violence potential were identified as such using data from a set of ages comparable to those during which they were identified as high-rate violent offenders.

Predictions of Odd and Even Rates

Although the arrest rates obtained for the odd and even ages were not particularly useful for identifying high-rate offenders based on the other half of their data, it was expected that the inclusion of other information about the offenders might enable us to predict those rates with greater accuracy. Using the data for the entire follow-up period, multiple regressions were employed to assess the extent to which all the information for the even half (plus background data) could predict total and violent arrest rates for the odd half, and *vice versa*. The sample was split in half so that predictive usefulness of each solution could be assessed on a different sample. In all, four stepwise regressions were run, predicting odd rates and even rates for both halves of the sample. Arrest rate variables were entered first, followed by the drug use, family status, and employment variables as a group. Background variables were entered next, with race entered only after all other eligible variables were included. The multiple correlation of the final equation was also calculated for the other half of the sample in each regression. Because data on drug use, marital status, employment, and family background were not available for all cases, means were substituted for missing data. There were 772 cases in one "half" of the sample and 811 in the other. The results are summarized below for rates of total arrests and violent arrests.

Average	Total Rate	Violent Rate
Multiple R	.755	.586
Multiple R^2	.570	.344
Multiple R (x-validation)	.742	.568

As shown, these regression accounted for about 57% of the variance in total arrest rates and 34% of the variance in violent arrest rates. In these half-samples, the bivariate correlation of the total arrest rate variables was about .70, and the correlation of the violent arrest rate variables was about .40; these rates alone could explain 49% and 16% of the variance in the rates for the corresponding (odd or even) rates. For total offenses, the addition of other variables improved these predictions only marginally. For violent arrest rates, greater improvement resulted from including other variables (doubling the explained variation). Still, the predictability of these rates was relatively low, suggesting that the low reliability of the arrest-rate measure placed severe constraints on the ability to predict arrest rates in this sample.

While these analyses did not help much in resolving the problem of predictability, given low reliabilities, they shed some light on the factors associated with high arrest rates during the course of a career. Consistent predictors of total arrest rates (found in three of the four final equations) were (a) the total arrest rate in the other half (odd or even years); (b) the rate of violent arrests (a negative effect, once the total rate was accounted for), (c) the percentage of time in the other half spent incarcerated, and (d) the percentage of time using hallucinogenic drugs. In other words, those with the highest rates in either the odd or even ages tended to have higher total rates in the other ages, lower violent arrest rates, less street tme, and more time using marijuana, LSD, mescaline, and other hallucinogenic drugs. For violent arrest rates, the consistent predictors included (a) the violent arrest rate in the other half; (b) the percent of time incarcerated; (c) hallucinogenic drug use; and (d) race (white offenders had lower rates).

In all, these solutions are not very enlightening about the factors related to relatively high criminal behavior rates in this sample. Most of the consistent predictors found in the above analyses were additional indicators of criminality (time incarcerated, for example). Thus, except for the importance of drug use as a correlate of criminal behavior, these analyses merely indicate that crime predicts crime. This suggests that at this level of risk for continued criminal behavior, little actually differentiates the offenders with the highest rates of arrest from those with lower rates. However, other factors may come into play when predicting from one time period to the next.

In the next section, some of the implications of these low reliabilities for the study of offense rate stability and prediction of offense behavior will be discussed.

Implications of Using Official Offense Measures

The stability of offense rates over time will be addressed, in the chapters that follow, both through studying the correlations of arrest rates for different time periods (four-year age blocks) and the extent of agreement (correspondence) between the categorized levels based on those rates from one period to the next. The foregoing findings will inform these analyses in two ways. First, they suggest that there is an upper limit to the expected correlations and rates of agreement that would be obtained for these four-year periods even if the underlying rates were reasonably stable. That upper limit for correlations is in the neighborhood of .60 for the total arrest rate and .30 for the violent arrest rate. For rates of correspondence, the upper limit for high-rate to high-rate agreement for total arrest rates is about 61%, and for *any* violent arrest about 51%. Indicators of stability over time must be judged against these "natural" limits imposed by the data. Second, they suggest that little improvement over simple, commonly used methods (using logarithms) could be expected by manipulating the data (truncating or eliminating high scores) or by excluding certain kinds of cases from the analysis. The analyses in the following chapters will therefore include all cases for whom data were available (for four-year blocks, a minimum of 12 months of street time was still required).

For predictions, these data also suggest upper limits to the predictability of offense rates over time. The present findings suggest that even if offense behavior were not to change over time, the best predictions based on arrest data covering as much as 10 years would account for around half (53%) of the variance in subsequent total arrest rates for these high-risk offenders. Explained variation in violent arrest rates would be expected to be considerably less—around 20%. The inclusion of other predictors in the equations did tend to increase the explained variation to some extent, but it is unlikely that substantial increases would be found when predicting rates during one time period from information for previous periods. Even with the inclusion of additional variables, the explained variation in total arrest rates was less than 60%, and the explained variation in violent arrest rates was under 35%.

Over four-year periods, even less predictability of arrest rates would be expected. Under similar assumptions of behavioral stability, predictions of rates over four years, using the previous four-year rate, would account for only about 36% of the variance (the square of the average correlation for the four-year analyses, .597). For violent rates, the explained variation was only 8.7% (.295 squared). Future studies attempting to predict rates of criminal behavior using data available from official sources will have to keep in mind that there are upper limits to the predictability of these rates and that the upper limit is not very high when only a few years of data are available.

Chapter 6
Stability of Individual Arrest Rates

As discussed in the Introduction, the assumption of stability in criminal behavior is central both to current arguments in favor of selective incapacitation policies and to existing methods for estimating their probable benefits. The idea that certain offenders will commit crimes at very high rates whenever they are free to do so (not incarcerated) spawned the belief that scarce public resources could be most effectively applied to ensuring that those offenders remain behind bars longer than others. The assumption here is that the propensity to commit crimes is an enduring characteristic of the individual and that the propensity will express itself in terms of stable rates of criminal behavior under varying social and environmental conditions as long as the offender is active in crime (throughout his "career"). This assumption suggests that longer sentences for high-rate offenders (who, because of their high criminality, deserve longer sentences anyway) will have the most crime-reduction benefit in the future. While some instability in offense behavior would not reduce the potency of such an argument, considerable instability would suggest a more tenuous link between past and future behavior, reducing the likely payoff for incapacitating known high-rate offenders. Reduced certainty in the stability of offense behavior would also cast some doubt on the currently popular conception of criminal careers as stable patterns of criminal behavior.

The assumption of stability also lies at the foundation of most efforts to estimate the likely benefits of selective incapacitation policies. As discussed previously, models of the criminal justice system, developed by Shinnar and Shinnar (1975), have been used to estimate the likely effects of changing various characteristics of that system, including the lengths of prison terms for certain offenders (Cohen, 1978; Chaiken and Rolph, 1978; Greenwood, 1982). For heuristic purposes, these models have generally assumed that individual offense rates do not change over time. Although systematic changes, as in the decline by age found earlier, could presumably be incorporated, substantial instability would call into question the usefulness of these models. Thus, while the possible benefits of selective incapacitation policies do not *require* that offense rates be perfectly stable for individual offenders, the appeal of these policies and the estimation of their likely effects have been grounded firmly on this assumption of stability.

The analyses in Chapters 3 and 4 showed that, for these high-risk offenders, both the participation in crime (judged by any arrest) and the rate of arrest for the sample as a whole and for various subsamples showed definite declines with age. These trends suggest that social and environmental factors have a strong role in determining the year-to-year extent of criminality among offenders, and that the type, number, or importance of these factors change with age. Further, the decline in arrest rates was most marked for those offenders with the highest arrest rates at ages 18 to 19, suggesting that factors operating to inhibit criminal behavior may well apply differentially, with the highest-rate offenders most affected.[1]

It should be noted, however, that because these analyses used rates of arrest aggregated across all members of the sample (or subsample) in question, they masked individual differences in rates and their change (or stability) over time. As such, those analyses could not address the extent of either (a) *relative stability*—whether offenders maintain constant relative rates of arrest over time (do high-rate offenders at age 21 have higher rates of arrest than other offenders as they all got older?); or, (b) *absolute stability*—whether some offenders' rates defy the general downward trend with age and remain at the same level over time. Both issues are important for understanding the possible benefits of selective incapacitation policies, as well as for understanding criminal behavior in general.

If relative rates of arrest within age groups are stable (even though the rate may decline with age), it may still make sense to select out the higher rate offenders for increased sentences. However, the crime-reduction benefits associated with increased incarceration for particular offenders would depend on their age and prior offense rate. It could be, for example, that a greater benefit would be derived from incapacitating medium-rate offenders at age 20 than from incapacitating high-rate offenders once they reach age 30. Policy decisions concerning whether or not to increase the sentences of particular offenders would thus depend on their previous rate of arrest, the age at which they would ordinarily be freed, and the expected rate of decline for offenders *with that rate of arrest at that age.* Further, the estimation of the *overall* effect of the policy would have to take into account differences in age, sentence length, rates of prior arrest, and age-by-rate-specific declines in arrest rates for the various mixes of offenders to whom the policy may be applied. All these factors would have to be taken into account in addition to the estimated probabilities of arrest, conviction, and incarceration (which may also differ

---

[1] An alternative explanation might be that these rates were spuriously high due to measurement error, and that they would naturally fall toward the average values for the larger sample. Such rate drops, however, would be expected to be sudden, rather than gradual, since the measurement error would, presumably, not affect the same offenders in the same way over different time periods.

for different types of offenders). Of course, the ability to adequately estimate these benefits for individuals or overall would decrease to the extent that these relative rates are not stable over time.

Policy issues aside, it is still important to better understand the stability of relative rates of arrest over time. Attempts to understand differential rates of offending in terms of the attributes of *offenders* (family backgrounds, psychological characteristics, etc.) obviously make the most sense if offenders maintain their rates of behavior relative to one another. High-rate offenders, in this sense, could be reasonably assumed to be "different." If, on the other hand, these rates are not stable, then high-rate offenders at one point in time would be a different group than high-rate offenders at another. Attempts to understand what causes high rates of offending would be better off searching for *situational* factors common to these groups. In other words, general instability would suggest that differences in rates of offending are as much the result of situational (social and environmental) factors, which can be understood to vary across offenders *over time and place*, as they are the result of enduring differences in criminal propensity.

It is also possible that the downward trend in arrest rates did not apply to all offenders equally. In other words, in spite of the general trends, there may still have been a core of high-rate offenders who maintained relatively constant (and high) rates of criminal behavior over time and who, in spite of measurement error in arrest rates, could be identified as such. Offenders of this type would constitute an important sample of those generally considered to be prime candidates for selective intervention efforts; they are, in fact, the very offenders on whose existence the notion of selective incapacitation has been based. For selective incapactitation to work, after all, it is necessary not only to be able to posit the existence of a core of stable high-rate offenders, but also to be able to identify them. Thus, if offenders who maintain high levels of arrests are particularly rare, constituting only a fraction of the offenders who have high rates of arrest at any point in time, the identification of targets for selective incapacitation would certainly be problematic.

The investigation of offense-rate stability in this sample was approached in several ways. First correlations between arrest rates calculated over four-year age blocks were used[2] to assess the extent of *relative stability*. These correlations were compared to one another and to the correlation obtained for arrest rates based on sets of four odd and four even ages. To investigate *absolute stability*, arrest rates were collapsed into low, medium, and high. The categorized rates were used to calculate transitional probabilities for high-rate offenders and to establish overall career patterns (over three or four age blocks). These latter analyses will point to the effects on individual arrest rates

---

[2] Again, four-year blocks were chosen to overcome some of the instability in rate estimation that would result from measurement error over short time periods. Rates were calculated for all individuals who had at least 12 months of street time during the four-year period.

of the factors discussed to that point: general declines with age, instability of arrest rates due to measurement error, and any instability in these rates attributable to the changeable nature of criminal behavior over time.

Correlations of Age-Block Arrest Rates

Correlations among variables indicate the extent to which values for the same individual tend to be similarly high or low, as compared to those of other individuals. They are calculated relative to the means of the variables, taking into account the overall variation of each.[3] Thus, the correlations between rates for different time periods take into account overall declines by age and the effect of these declines on the distribution of rates, thereby providing an indication of the stability of those rates relative to other offenders. The findings in Chapter 5 indicated that, due to measurement error, the correlations of arrest rates would be expected to be considerably less than perfect even if the underlying offense rates were fairly stable. For rates calculated on the basis of four years of data, expected correlations were estimated to be around .60 for total offenses and .30 for violent offenses. Interpretation of the present correlations will be in terms of these "standards" for the arrest rate correlations: lower correlations would suggest that the rates actually varied over time for the individuals in this sample.

The correlations for the five four-year age blocks from age 18 to age 37 are shown in Table 6.1. Also included are the correlations between the rates for these age blocks and the rate based on all available adult data for each offender. For total offenses, the highest correlations among age-block rates were between adjacent blocks. For nonadjacent age blocks, the correlation decreased as the time between the two age blocks increased. None of the correlations reached the .60 standard for stability, although the correlation beween the rate for the 30 to 33 block and that for the 34 to 37 block approached that level. These findings suggest that, for total offenses, the rates of arrest were not completely stable and that the greatest stability occurred over the short run. For violent offenses, a similar pattern was found. Correlations, in general, did not reach the standard (.30) and decreased as the time between the age blocks increased.[4] However, all these correlations were

---

[3] Because of the sensitivity of the means and the variance estimates to extreme values, the natural logarithm of each rate variable was used, rather than the rate itself.

[4] Similar analyses involving only "active" periods or including only those cases with one or more offenses (total or violent) showed nearly identical patterns of correlations. The correlations were generally lower, and showed similar decreases as the time period increased; these findings suggest that these patterns were not due to some offenders having ended their careers while others continued or to the inclusion (especially for violent offenses) of a considerable number of offenders with "zero" rates (no offenses) in every block.

TABLE 6.1 Arrest-rate correlations: Four-year age blocks.

	18–21	22–25	26–29	30–33	34–37
Total Offenses					
22–25	.482[a]				
26–29	.372	.508			
30–33	.226	.331	.506		
34–37	.145	.289	.344	.577	
18–37	.753	.798	.737	.654	.545
Violent Offenses					
22–25	.2401				
26–29	.252	.256			
30–33	.222	.162	.286		
34–37	.119	.197	.170	.206	
18–37	.674	.710	.672	.635	.479

Note: Correlations include cases with at least 12 months of street time for both age-blocks (minimum $n = 504$). The natural logarithm of all variables was used.
[a] All correlations significant ($p < .01$).

statistically significant, meaning that there was, most likely, a relationship between an individual's rate at any point in time (relative to others) and his rate at other points in time. Thus, while relatively high-rate offenders tended to remain so, there was a clear departure from overall stability. The correlations of each of the block rates with the rate for the total follow-up (18–37) suggest that the arrest rates over the period from age 22 to age 25 were most indicative of how these offenders differed from one another over the entire 20-year period.

To better understand the effect of increased time between measurements, rates were calculated for each four-year period from age 18 to age 33, incremented by one year at a time. The correlations among these rates are shown in Table 6.2. Reading down the columns, each correlation is between rates for four-year blocks one year later than the one above it. For total offenses, the following pattern was observed: the greater the time between the two four-year blocks, the lower the correlation between the two rates. These patterns suggest that while offense behavior is not totally unstable, changing drastically over time, it does change, with some offenders showing an increase in offense behavior and others showing a decrease relative to one another. The greater the time between the period of observation and the period of interest, the less useful the observed arrest rate would be for predicting later differences in these rates.

For violent offenses, no clear pattern emerged. There was a similar tendency for correlations to decrease with increasing time intervals between periods, but the decrease was not as pronounced. In fact, some correlations were higher than for immediately adjacent periods, suggesting that, overall, rates of violent offenses may be somewhat more stable than rates for all offenses combined.

TABLE 6.2 Arrest-rate correlations: Four-year age blocks incremented by one year.

	18–21	19–22	20–23	21–24	22–25
Total Offenses					
22–25	.482[a]				
23–26	.440	.488			
24–27	.400	.445	.503		
25–28	.378	.414	.463	.499	
26–29	.372	.419	.464	.483	.508
27–30	.329	.367	.418	.426	.448
28–31	.316	.350	.393	.391	.396
29–32	.270	.302	.350	.340	.351
30–33	.226	.262	.323	.321	.331
Violent Offenses					
22–25	.240				
23–26	.221	.186			
24–27	.228	.223	.230		
25–28	.255	.235	.223	.222	
26–29	.252	.296	.289	.263	.256
27–30	.230	.275	.257	.233	.233
28–31	.189	.232	.200	.169	.152
29–32	.210	.220	.216	.184	.165
30–33	.222	.226	.219	.171	.162

Note: The natural logarithm of all variables was used.
[a] All correlations significant ($p < .01$).

TABLE 6.3 Arrest-rate correlations: Eight-year age blocks.

	18–25	22–29	18–37
Total Offenses			
26–33	.470[a]		.791
30–37	.352	.486	.730
18–37	.889	.868	1.00
Violent Offenses			
26–33	.358		.759
30–37	.280	.340	.743
18–37	.857	.827	1.00

Note: Correlations include cases with at least 12 months of street time for both age blocks. The natural logarithm of all variables was used.
[a] All correlations significant ($p < .01$).

However, the correlations were all fairly low (as was the correlation for odd and even four-year rates), suggesting that, for practical purposes, any predictive benefit based on higher stability was more than offset by measurement problems for these low-base-rate offenses.

Additional evidence of instability in arrest rates was found when adjacent age blocks were combined to create eight-year rates of arrest for total and violent offenses. As shown in Table 6.3, the correlations between adjacent age blocks again were highest, with considerable decreases occurring for the correlations involving age blocks separated by four years. Of interest in this table are the relatively low correlations, even among the adjacent eight-year blocks. These eight-year rates should provide more stable indications of an individuals's "true" arrest rate over those periods, the larger time frame mitigating, to some extent, the problem of measurement error. (This contention is supported by their higher correlations with the overall adult rate.) If offense rates were stable and the main problem was one of measurement error, these eight-year correlations would be expected to be much higher than those obtained for four-year blocks. For total offenses, the arrest rate correlations were about the same as for the four-year blocks. The most likely explanation for this similarity is that whatever advantage is gained from using longer time periods in terms of decreased measurement error is offset by the inclusion in these rates of time periods that are increasingly dissimilar in *actual* offense rates (earlier behavior included in one rate and later behavior in the other). For violent offenses, some increase in the correlations was found, again suggesting that the underlying offense rates may have been more stable over time. However, the increase in correlations resulting from decreased measurement error is not completely offset by increased diversity in actual behavior.

Overall, then, these correlational analyses suggest that offense behavior was not stable over the careers of these individual offenders. Although some lack of perfect correlation between rates would have been expected even if rates were stable over time, the actual correlations were lower than would be expected basel on measurement error alone. Further, the longer the time period between measurements, the greater the discrepancy between the actual and expected correlations. Although a reasonable relationship was found between rates for any two periods of time, these relationships were not great enough to warrant the assumption that rates of individual offending were stable, relative to other offenders. Rates of arrest for violent offenses, which were found earlier to be more affected by measurement error, appeared to be somewhat more stable over time, but even for these offenses, stability was not high.

Patterns of Arrest-Rate Levels

To investigate the patterns of arrest-rate levels over time, the rates for each four-year age block were collapsed into low, medium, and high using the same cut-offs for each age block. A single standard allowed the identification of patterns of change in the actual rates, ignoring the general decline in these rates by age. The cut-off points were derived from the distribution of rates calculated for the entire follow-up period and chosen so as to divide that overall distribution into rough thirds. Because the rates based on the four-year blocks are affected by the overall decline in rates by age, these cut-off points would not be expected to divide the sample into thirds for each age block; for later blocks, the proportion of cases with lower rates would be expected to increase and the proportion of cases with higher rates would be expected to decrease.

Two types of analysis were performed using these collapsed variables. The first focused on the transitional probabilities for high-rate arrestees: the probabilities that high-rate arrestees showed low, medium, or high rates of arrest in the next age block. The second type of analysis involved global patterns over the entire follow-up period, focusing on the first three or four blocks in which the offenders had valid rates (had at least 12 months of street time). The transitional probabilites allow for understanding the usefulness of prior rates for predicting subsequent rates of arrest, while the global patterns suggest the extent of variability in these rates over the entire career.

Transitional Probabilities for High-Rate Arrestees

The first set of analysis were intended to provide information on the expected distribution of the arrest-rate levels of high-rate offenders in those blocks following the block in which they were identified as high-rate offenders. Because of the combined effects of measurement error, declining rates over time, and general instability, one would not expect a very high proportion of high-rate arrestees to remain so in subsequent age blocks. In addition, some high-rate arrestees spent enough of the next age block incarcerated that they did not have the requisite 12 months of street time on which to base an adequate estimate of their arrest rates. Thus, the present analysis points to the tendency of offenders who had high rates of arrest in one period *and* who managed to accumulate 12 months of street time in the next block to have various levels of arrest in that subsequent four-year block.

The transitional probabilities for high-rate arrestees and others are shown in Table 6.4. For each block, the number and percentage of the high-rate arrestees having low, medium, or high rates of arrest in the next block are provided first. Immediately below these figures are those for the non-high-rate arrestees and the entire sample. For example, of the 1302 offenders with valid rates in the 18 to 21 block and the 22 to 25 block, 576 (44.2%) had low rates of arrest in the 22 to 25 block, 280 (21.5%) had medium rates, and 446 (34.3%) had high rates. Of the 618 high-rate offenders among the 18 to 21 year olds, 167 (27.0%) had low rates during the 22 to 25 block, 141 (22.8%) had medium rates, and 310 (50.2%) had high rates of arrest.

Consistent with expectations, these figures show that the proportion of cases with high rates was lower for each succeeding age block. For high-rate

TABLE 6.4 Transitional probabilities for high-rate offenders

Block	Number (%)	Next block		
		Low	Medium	High
Total Offenses				
18–21: High-rate	618 (47.5%)	167 (27.0%)	141 (22.8%)	310 (50.2%)
Others	684 (52.5%)	409 (59.8%)	139 (20.3%)	136 (19.9%)
Total	1302 (100%)	576 (44.2%)	280 (21.5%)	446 (34.3%)
22–25: High-rate	348 (30.1%)	115 (33.0%)	87 (25.0%)	146 (42.0%)
Others	809 (69.9%)	610 (75.4%)	125 (15.5%)	74 (9.1%)
Total	1157 (100%)	725 (62.7%)	212 (18.3%)	220 (19.0%)
26–29: High-rate	153 (16.0%)	63 (41.2%)	36 (23.5%)	54 (35.3%)
Others	806 (84.0%)	679 (84.2%)	78 (9.6%)	49 (6.1%)
Total	959 (100%)	742 (77.4%)	114 (11.9%)	103 (10.7%)
30–33: High-rate	54 (9.4%)	17 (31.5%)	15 (27.8%)	22 (40.7%)
Others	519 (90.6%)	451 (86.9%)	48 (9.2%)	20 (3.8%)
Total	573 (100%)	468 (81.7%)	63 (11.0%)	42 (7.3%)
Violent Offenses				
18–21: High rate	433 (33.3%)	214 (49.4%)	38 (8.8%)	181 (41.1%)
Others	869 (66.7%)	600 (69.0%)	81 (9.3%)	188 (21.6%)
Total	1302 (100%)	814 (62.5%)	119 (9.1%)	369 (28.3%)
22–25: High-rate	286 (24.7%)	176 (61.5%)	25 (8.7%)	85 (29.7%)
Others	871 (75.3%)	684 (78.5%)	60 (6.9%)	127 (14.6%)
Total	1157 (100%)	860 (74.3%)	85 (7.3%)	212 (18.3%)
26–29: High-rate	159 (16.6%)	99 (62.3%)	8 (5.0%)	52 (32.7%)
Others	800 (83.4%)	689 (86.1%)	32 (4.0%)	79 (9.9%)
Total	959 (100%)	788 (82.2%)	40 (4.2%)	131 (13.7%)
30–33: High-rate	80 (14.0%)	59 (73.8%)	0 (0.0%)	21 (26.3%)
Others	493 (86.0%)	459 (93.1%)	3 (0.6%)	31 (6.3%)
Total	573 (100%)	518 (90.4%)	3 (0.5%)	52 (9.1%)

Note: The following cut-offs were used:

	Total	Violent
Low	0–.79	0
Medium	.80–2.09	.01–.30
High	2.10 +	.31 +

arrestees, the proportion of *high-rate* offenders with high rates in the next block also decreases somewhat after the first transition, but then appears to stabilize at around 40% for total offenses and about 30% for violent offenses. For each age block, the proportion of high-rate arrestees who had high rates of arrest in the next block was considerably higher than for others, indicating some stability in these patterns. For all except the first transition for total offenses, however, less than half maintained high arrest rates into the next block. For total offenses, it is interesting to note that for each transition, high-rate offenders were only slightly less likely to have low rates of arrest in the next block as to maintain high levels. For violent offenses, low (zero) rates of arrest were the most likely for high-rate arrestees as well as for all other members of the sample. For no transition did half of the high-rate arrestees have *any* violent arrests in the next age block.

To assess the added power of additional information on arrest rate stability, the same transitional probabilities were calculated for those cases that had high rates of arrest in the previous *two* age blocks. That is, for cases with valid rates in the 18 to 21, 22 to 25, and 26 to 29 blocks, transitional probabilities during the 26 to 29 block were calculated for those cases with

TABLE 6.5 Transitional probabilities for high-rate offenders over the previous two blocks (high in both)

		Next block		
Block	Number (%)	Low	Medium	High
Total Offenses				
18–21/22–25				
High-rate	226 (20.1%)	64 (28.3%)	53 (23.5%)	109 (48.2%)
Others	899 (79.9%)	646 (71.9%)	150 (16.7%)	103 (11.5%)
Total	1125 (100%)	710 (63.1%)	203 (18.0%)	212 (18.8%)
22–25/26–29				
High-rate	77 (9.0%)	27 (35.1%)	19 (24.7%)	31 (40.3%)
Others	778 (9.10%)	648 (83.3%)	76 (9.8%)	54 (6.9%)
Total	855 (100%)	675 (78.9%)	95 (11.1%)	85 (9.9%)
26–29/30–33				
High-rate	22 (4.2%)	7 (31.8%)	3 (13.6%)	12 (54.5%)
Others	503 (95.8%)	428 (85.1%)	50 (9.9%)	25 (5.0%)
Total	525 (100%)	435 (82.9%)	53 (10.1%)	37 (7.0%)
Violent Offenses				
18–21/22–25				
High-rate	126 (11.2%)	72 (57.1%)	7 (5.6%)	47 (37.3%)
Others	999 (88.8%)	768 (76.8%)	76 (7.6%)	155 (15.5%)
Total	1125 (100%)	840 (74.7%)	83 (7.4%)	202 (18.0%)
22–25/26–29				
High-rate .	44 (5.1%)	29 (65.9%)	13 (6.8%)	12 (27.3%)
Others	811 (94.9%)	686 (84.6%)	20 (2.5%)	95 (11.7%)
Total	855 (100%)	715 (83.6%)	33 (3.9%)	107 (12.5%)
26–29/30–33				
High-rate	28 (5.3%)	17 (66.5%)	0 (0.0%)	11 (39.3%)
Others	497 (94.7%)	461 (92.8%)	2 (0.4%)	34 (6.8%)
Total	525 (100%)	478 (91.0%)	2 (0.4%)	45 (8.6%)

Note: The following cut-offs were used:

	Total	Violent
Low	0–.79	0
Medium	.80–2.09	.01–.30
High	2.10 +	.31 +

high rates of arrest in both the 18 to 21 and 22 to 25 blocks. It was hypothesized that a stable pattern of high arrests over two blocks might establish a pattern that held through the next block as well. However, as shown in Table 6.5, the percentages of these two-block, high-rate arrestees who had high rates of arrest in the next block were only slightly higher than that found when only the rate for the immediately prior block was considered. Further, all the percentages (except for the last transition, where very small numbers were involved) were below 50%. These offenders were still nearly as likely to have low rates of arrest as high rates for total offenses, and *more* likely to have *zero* rates than high rates for violent offenses.

Thus, knowing that offenders in this sample maintained high rates of arrest over two four-year periods did not substantially increase the probability that they would have a high rates of arrest in the next four-year period. Using apparent stability as the criterion for identifying cases as high-rate offenders during the 26 to 29 age block, the identification would have been correct in 109 cases and wrong (false positives) in 117 cases (51.8%). It would also have mistakenly identified 103 (11.5%) of the 899 non-high-rate arrestes as non-high-rate in the next block when they actually were high-rate—false negatives. Note that these 103 offenders constituted almost half (48.5%) of the 212 high-rate arrestees during ages 26 to 29. Thus, while the false-negative rate was fairly low, both the false-positive rate and the percentage of high-rate arrestees not identified on the basis of earlier rates would have been higher than the true-positive rate of 48.2%. Predictions for the other age blocks showed similar results.

From the figures in this table, the proportion of the sample remaining high-rate through three age blocks can be easily calculated. For total offenses, the number of cases with high arrest rates through ages 18 to 21, 22 to 25, and 26 to 29 was 109. By dividing this number by the total number of cases with valid rates through these three age blocks (1125), the percentage of cases who remained high-rate from ages 18 to 29 can be obtained: 109/1125 = 9.7%. Similar calculations show that for the three age blocks between ages 22 and 33, the percentage with all high rates was 3.6%, and for the blocks between ages 26 and 34, 2.3% had high rates in all three periods. For violent offenses, the percentages for the three three-block periods were 4.2%, 1.4%, and 2.1%, respectively. Clearly, the maintenance of high rates of offenses through three four-year age blocks in a row was quite rare. This small group of offenders, who presumably would be the most appropriate focus of selective incapacitation policies, would constitute a small target indeed. Hitting such a target would be a considerable challenge for any prediction device.

It must be remembered, of course, that these results cannot be taken as accurate indications of the extent of true stability in criminal behavior, for at least two reasons. First, measurement error may attenuate actual relationships, masking some of the actual stability in these rates; some proportion of those cases with high rates over two blocks may have had high rates of criminal *behavior* in the next block, while only having relatively low rates of *arrest*. Second, it is possible that some offenders with high rates of arrest spent enough of the next adjacent block incarcerated that they did not accumulate the requisite 12 months of street time for a valid rate calculation. These offenders may have had high arrest rates in that block if they were free to do so. Thus, although these transitional probabilities suggest serious problems for selective incapacitation policies, it is not possible to infer from these data actual incapacitation effects, in terms of the actual proportion of high-rate offenders identifiable on the basis of apparent stability to that point. It would appear, however, that the combined effects of measurement error, declines in criminal behavior with age, and instability in offense behavior minimize the likelihood of observing patterns of continued high rates of arrests among even these high-risk offenders.

Global Patterns of Arrest-Rate Levels

To further explore the nature of stability and change in arrest rates over the careers of these offenders, an attempt was made to develop a single index that would indicate the overall pattern of arrest-rate levels for each individual. In order to focus clearly on patterns of arrest during periods in which the offenders were free to be arrested, these analyses concentrated only on blocks in which offenders had *valid* age-block rates. In other words, those periods in whch an offender did not have 12 months of street time due to incarceration were ignored. For example, if an offender did not have a valid rate for the 22 to 25 age block, the rate for the following age blocks were moved forward; this process continued until the rates for the valid blocks were arranged sequentially. Rate levels were established using the same cut-off points as in the previous analyses of transitional probabilities.

These rate levels were first used to establish a single three-digit or four-digit number made up of the levels for each block. For instance, an offender that had medium rates of arrest over the first three valid blocks would have received an index number of 222 for the three-block analysis (only those cases with at least three valid blocks were included). If that same offender dropped to low-rate during the fourth block, his index number would be 2221 for the four-block analysis; if he had no valid fourth block, he would not have received a number (and would have been included only in the three-block analysis). In this way, a single number would provide information on the overall pattern of rate levels over those blocks for each offender in which he was on the street long enough to have an arrest rate calculated. There were a total of 1316 offenders in the three-block analyses and 968 offenders in the four-block analyses.

For the three-block analyses, there were a total of 3^3, or 27 possible combinations of the three levels. For both total offenses and violent offenses, all 27 possible patterns were represented in the sample. For total offenses, the most common patterns included the following.

Pattern	Number	Percent
111	219	16.6%
211	146	11.1%
311	144	10.9%
333	126	9.6%

Thus, included among the four most common patterns were stable low-rate and stable high-rate patterns. There were only 21 offenders (1.6% of the sample) with stable patterns of medium-level arrest rates. For violent offenses, the most common patterns included:

Pattern	Number	Percent
111	459	34.9%
311	162	12.3%
331	104	7.9%
131	102	7.8%

The predominant pattern, as expected, was no violent arrests in any block (34.9%). Those with stable patterns of medium-rate and high-rate arrests constituted only 0.3% and 4.8% of the sample, respectively.

For the four-block analyses, 3^4, or 81 patterns were possible. For total offenses, there were 71 patterns (87.7% of those possible) represented in the sample, with the most common patterns being

Pattern	Number	Percent
1111	165	17.0%
2111	113	11.7%
3111	106	11.0%
3211	57	5.9%

The common patterns show a marked similarity to those found for three blocks: a low or declining pattern of arrest over time. Sustained patterns of high-rate arrests (2.8%) or medium-rate arrests (0.7%) were extremely rare over four age blocks.

For violent offenses, 63 patterns (77.8% of those possible) emerged. For these offenses, the mot common patterns included:

Pattern	Number	Percent
1111	347	35.8%
3111	112	11.6%
1311	60	6.2%
3311	57	5.9%

Thus, over half the offenders in the sample had either no arrests for violent offenses in any block or a high-rate of arrests for these offenses during the first valid block and none thereafter. Only 1.0% had four high-rate periods and *none* had four medium-rate periods.

The number of patterns that were found bespeaks the diversity of career lines among these offenders as well as the overall lack of stability in arrest rates. In reviewing these patterns, however, it was apparent that many patterns did not differ substantially. For example, the patterns 112, 121, and 211 may all be considered to indicate generally low rates of arrest overall. It was decided, therefore, to combine some of these patterns into more general categories reflecting the number of age blocks with low, medium, or high rates of arrest. These categories were further collapsed into categories indicating "mostly low," "mostly medium" and "mostly high" rates, based on having only one period with a different arrest-rate level (i.e., only one level different from the others). That difference, moreover, could only be from one level to the next (e.g., from low to medium, but not from low to high). Patterns that did not fit into these general categories were felt to be most indicative of instability.

Both sets of categories, for both total offenses and violent offenses, and for both the three-block analyses and the four-block analyses, are shown in Table 6.6. Note that for each analysis, the general category indicating the greatest instability in arrest rates (the "other" category) included the greatest number of cases. The next most common general category in each analyses was "mostly low." Only for the three-block analysis for total offenses did the number of cases in either the "mostly medium" or "mostly high" categories include 10% or more of the cases.

Comparing the three-block and four-block results for total offenses, the proportions of cases staying mostly low was about the same, while the proportion in the "other" category was substantially higher for the four-block analysis. Judging from the differences in the percentages in the more specific categories, it would appear that those cases with mostly medium or mostly high rates over three blocks did not maintain those levels over the fourth block. The proportion with three low and one high was about the same as for

TABLE 6.6 Arrest-rate patterns over valid age blocks.

	Total offenses				Violent offenses			
Pattern	N	%	N	%	N	%	N	%
Three Valid Blocks	1316				1316			
Mostly low:			419	31.8%			584	44.4%
3 low	219	16.6%			459	34.9%		
2 low, 1 med	210	16.0%			125	9.5%		
Mostly medium:			181	13.8%			35	2.7%
3 med	21	1.6%			4	.3%		
2 med, 1 low	181	6.2%			21	1.6%		
2 med, 1 high	179	6.0%			10	1.8%		
Mostly high:			249	18.9%			90	6.8%
3 high	126	9.6%			63	4.8%		
2 high, 1 med	123	9.3%			27	2.1%		
Other:			457	34.7%			607	46.1%
2 low, 1 high	168	12.8%			316	24.0%		
2 high, 1 low	117	8.9%			194	14.7%		
High, med, low	172	13.1%			97	7.4%		
Four Valid Blocks	968				968			
Mostly low:			318	32.9%			435	44.9%
4 low	165	17.0%			347	35.8%		
3 low, 1 med	153	15.8%			88	9.1%		
Mostly medium:			41	4.2%			5	.6%
4 med	7	.7%			0	—		
3 med, 1 low	15	1.5%			4	.4%		
3 med, 1 high	19	2.0%			1	.1%		
Mostly high:			65	6.7%			17	1.8%
4 high	27	2.8%			10	1.0%		
3 high, 1 med	38	3.9%			7	.7%		
Other:			544	56.2%			511	52.8%
3 low, 1 high	126	13.0%			210	21.7%		
2 med, 2 low	63	6.5%			21	2.2%		
3 high, 1 low	34	3.5%			50	5.2%		
2 high, 2 med	28	2.9%			4	.4%		
2 high, 2 low	62	6.4%			112	11.6%		
High, med, low	231	23.9%			114	11.8%		

Note: The following cut-offs were used:

	Total	Violent
Low	0–.79	0
Medium	.80–2.09	.01–.30
High	2.10$^+$	.31$^+$

two low and one high, while those indicating more diverse patterns, including the "high, medium, and low" category showed an increase. Thus, except for those offenders with stable low-rate arrest patterns, the longer the period over which these offenders were obseved, the more likely that they showed considerable variation in their arrest-rate patterns.

For violent offenses, stable patterns even over three blocks were rare, except for those with no violent arrests at all. In fact, it was rare for an offender to have *any* violent arrests in all three blocks: 104 offenders, out of 857 with one or more arrests for violent offenses. All other violent offenders had at least one four-year period (among those in which he was on the street at least 12 months) in which there were no arrests for violent crimes. Less than half the violent offenders (416 of 857) had two or more periods with violent arrests. Over four valid blocks, there were 621 offenders with any arrests for violent crimes. Of these, 298 (48.0%) had only one period in which such an arrest occurred, and at least 431 (69.4%) had two or more periods absent of any violent arrests (some proportion of the "high, medium, and low" category had two low periods). This high proportion with no-arrest periods made stable patterns of violent arrest rates unlikely.

Overall, the findings suggest that these offenders were unlikely to have stable patterns of arrest rates over their careers. These arrest rates were not completely *unstable*, of course, in the sense that behavior patterns were randomly distributed, but the extent of stability was considerably less than is implied in currently popular conceptions of criminal "careers" and less than would be necessary to justify selective incapacitation policies. Thus, while the rates over four-year blocks did have some usefulness for predicting the level of arrest rate during a subsequent period, at no point were the high-rate arrestees *likely* to have high rates of arrest during the next block. High rates during *two* blocks was only slightly more predictive of high rates in the next block. Analyses of overall patterns showed the variety of arrest-rate levels experienced by these offenders and the overall instability in the arrest rates over time. Again, these findings reflected the combined effects of maturation, measurement error in the arrest rates, and instability in the criminal behavior of these offenders. These effects, it would appear, severely limit the usefulness of official arrest data at any point in time for identifying those offenders who would be the most appropriate targets for selective incapacitation. Alone, the combined effects of maturation and instability would call into question the assumptions underlying the concept of selective incapacitation and would certainly create problems for attempts to estimate the potential effects of such a policy.

Chapter 7
Pre/Post Comparisons: Prison or Probation

The analysis of these offenders' arrest-rate patterns has thus far focused on the entire follow-up period or on somewhat arbitrary age blocks. Decisions regarding sentencing policy, however, must occur at particular points in these careers: at the point of sentencing. It is important, therefore, both to apply and to assess the applicability of these global patterns to the understanding of patterns observable at that important juncture. In this chapter, the results of analyses similar to those performed earlier using arrest data for the periods prior to and following a probation or prison sentence will be presented.

In general, the results show that all the general patterns described earlier applied to the presentence and postsentence periods as well: ethnic differences in aggregate arrest rates, a decline in arrest rates by age, and arrest rate instability at the individual level. In addition, two other trends observable at that particular point in time will be discussed: an escalation in aggregate arrest rates during the years immediately prior to the current sentence, and a greater-than-expected decline in these rates during those years immediately following release. These two trends add to the general instability of offense rates over that period, making arrest rates during the presentence period even less indicative of postrelease rates than earlier age blocks were of later ones. As a result, official data on criminality appear to be least useful for identifying differences in criminal propensity precisely at that point when they would most likely be employed.

The sample of interest in these analyses was that subset of cases for whom presentence investigation reports (PSIs) or prison reports were obtained. Recall that the supplementary samples obtained from probation departments and from the California Department of Corrections (CDC) were excluded from the analyses of overall career patterns (Chapter 3 and 4) because they were sampled on the basis of *having* certain patterns (adult probation or prison terms). For the present analyses, it is the periods of time before and after these sentences that are important, so it is appropriate to include these supplementary cases. Not included in these analyses, on the other hand, were those cases from the original CYA sample who did not serve adult prison terms and who did not have a recent probation report. As discussed in Chapter 2, prison reports were obtained for all cases in the CDC Supplementary sample ($n = 175$) and virtually all cases in the CYA cohort that went on to adult prison ($n = 492$).[1] Probation materials were obtained for cases placed on probation in the recent past (files are destroyed five years after a case is discharged from probation). The Probation Supplementary sample ($n = 98$) included cases randomly selected from those known to have been arrested for robbery or burglary, although the conviction offense in the present analyses may not have been for those crimes. These cases had no state-level incarcerations (juvenile or adult) prior to the conviction for which the PSIs were obtained. All cases in the CYA cohort with probation files were included ($n = 142$); these cases had no adult prison commitments.

Our interest was in four-year blocks of time prior to, and following, the conviction and related incarceration (if any). This conviction experience will be referred to as the "current sentence." Some cases had more than one PSI or prison report and the earliest conviction was chosen as the current sentence to maximize the number of cases with follow-up data. The "Pre" period included up to four years of available data prior to the sentence obtained (probation, probation with jail, or prison). This period was bounded on the bottom by age 18, limiting the length of the period for cases with early convictions. The "Post" period included up to four years of data after release from jail or prison (some "probation" cases had no incarceration, so that the Post period immediately followed the Pre period). This Post period was also divided into single years, and was bounded by the final follow-up date (or death) for each case. Data for periods prior to the Pre period and following the Post period were also obtained, allowing the calculation of rates for the entire adult career.[2]

For various reasons, not all cases were included in all analyses. Since only adult offense data were used, some cases who entered prison after barely reaching age 18 had no prior arrest information (three cases) or had too little street time during that period to allow adequate calculation of an arrest rate (two cases). A number of cases had no postrelease follow-up or too little street time after release for rate calculations. Cases with any prior or post-release data were included in aggregate rate calculations, however. As before, analyses focusing on rates for ethnic groups included only those cases classified as white, black, or Hispanic. A breakdown of the sample in terms of ethnicity and available data is provided in Appendix 1.

The Pre and Post data were analyzed both in terms of aggregate arrest rates

---

[1] Files were not found at CDC for a few cases in the CYA cohort, and file materials were not obtained for some cases who were still in CDC institutions (or active on parole) at the time of the data collection.

[2] As this data set was created, earlier errors in identifying final follow-up dates were corrected (see Chapter 4). As a result, these data do not exactly coincide with data used in earlier analyses. The errors were random, however, and should not affect any substantive conclusions or comparisons between trends found earlier and those obtained using the present data.

and individual rates of arrest. First, using aggregate data, arrest rates were calculated for the Pre period and the Post period by sample and ethnicity. These data provided a basis for assessing differences among these subgroups and for comparing rates prior to sentencing with those observed after release. Second, an assessment of the effects of age on the Post arrest rates for the cases with adult prison sentences was made. Next, to identify trends in arrest rates over the four-year periods prior to and following the current sentence, rates were calculated by sample for individual years during these four-year periods. Finally, the stability of individual arrest rates from Pre to Post was examined, using correlational analysis and Pre/post transitions.

Trends in Aggregate Arrest Rates

General Pre/Post Comparisons

Tables 7.1 and 7.2 show the rates of arrest for different general categories of crimes aggregated across ethnic groups and samples. Table 7.1 gives these rates for the period prior to the current sentence, and Table 7.2 shows the rates for the Post period. Since the rates for specific categories of offenses were not restricted to *participants*, they will reflect differences in participation in these crimes as well as in the rates of arrest. In particular, blacks and Hispanics in the sample were more likely to have arrests for violent offenses than whites; consequently, the arrest leading to probation/jail or prison was more likely to be a violent offense for these groups, and their Pre rates of violent arrests would be expected to be higher. Again, there are three comparisons of interest: among samples, among ethnic groups, and between Pre and Post.

The most striking difference in these tables is between Pre rates and Post rates, with the Post rates by sample being lower in all cases, and lower by ethnic group within sample in virtually all cases (a few of these rates did not decrease, but *none* showed a substantial increase). The greatest decreases were noted for those offenses for which rates were highest during the Pre period. Note that the Pre rates may be somewhat inflated, since each offender had to have at least one arrest during that period (for one type of crime or another). These arrests, however, are part of each offender's behavior during that period and cannot simply be ignored. Some reduction in rates from Pre to Post would be expected even if criminal behavior did not change. Further, given the earlier findings (Chapter 4) that these aggregate rates decreased with age and that this decrease was greatest for those cases with the highest early rates, these results may be due, in part, to maturation.

Among samples, there were clear differences between the cases who went to adult prison and those who did not for all offenses and for both the Pre and Post periods. In general, the two CDC samples and the two Probation samples were more similar to one another than CDC cases were to Probation cases, especially for the more serious offenses. For total offenses, there was a striking

TABLE 7.1 Aggregate yearly arrest rates by race and sample: Four-year pre period.

Offense type ethnicity	CYA/Prob	CYA/CDC	Suppl/Prob	Suppl/CDC
Total				
White	2.79	4.81	1.14	3.56
Black	2.57	5.17	1.80	3.61
Hispanic	2.92	4.66	1.33	3.91
Total	2.76	4.91	1.41	3.63
Violent				
White	.21	.55	.23	.70
Black	.39	1.23	.40	1.15
Hispanic	.40	.67	.18	.82
Total	.28	.82	.27	.89
Violent-aggressive				
White	.15	.31	.09	.37
Black	.23	.55	.18	.49
Hispanic	.34	.40	.10	.59
Total	.20	.41	.12	.45
Violent-economic				
White	.06	.25	.14	.32
Black	.16	.69	.21	.66
Hispanic	.06	.28	.08	.23
Total	.08	.41	.15	.44
Property				
White	.61	1.09	.41	1.09
Black	.50	1.32	.45	1.00
Hispanic	.52	.92	.41	1.00
Total	.57	1.14	.42	1.04

rank order among these groups, with CYA/CDC cases having the highest rates, followed by the Supplementary CDC cases, the CYA/Probation cases, and the Supplementary Probation cases, in that order. Further, while the rates for all groups were lower during the Post period, the same general rank order was maintained. For more specific types of offenses, the two CDC groups were more similar, and while the probation groups still showed differences, they were more similar to one another than to the CDC groups.

Rates by ethnic group indicate a greater similarity in arrest rates for total offenses than was found for the CYA cohort (all active offenders), suggesting that similar kinds of cases are selected by the justice system at various levels. With a few exceptions (property crimes), the direction of the differences in these rates resemble those found for the entire CYA cohort when all active cases were included. These differences reflect, in part, the fact that a greater proportion of blacks were sentenced for violent crimes, and would thus be expected to have higher rates of violent arrests during the Pre period. In the Post period, rates went down for almost all groups, and the differences in

TABLE 7.2 Aggregate yearly arrest rates by race and sample four-year post period.

Offense Type Ethnicity	CYA/Prob	CYA/CDC	Suppl/Prob	Suppl/CDC
Total				
White	1.47	2.33	.68	1.86
Black	1.44	2.65	1.47	2.41
Hispanic	1.51	2.68	1.03	2.30
Total	1.47	2.51	1.05	2.13
Violent				
White	.22	.37	.06	.35
Black	.25	.62	.12	.74
Hispanic	.12	.59	.28	.47
Total	.21	.50	.15	.51
Violent-aggressive				
White	.17	.18	.02	.15
Black	.19	.29	.12	.29
Hispanic	.05	.31	.08	.24
Total	.16	.24	.08	.21
Violent-economic				
Wite	.04	.19	.04	.20
Black	.06	.33	.10	.46
Hispanic	.05	.28	.10	.24
Total	.05	.26	.08	.30
Property				
White	.26	.63	.26	.64
Black	.17	.71	.34	.60
Hispanic	.24	.53	.20	.74
Total	.23	.64	.28	.64

rates were reduced somewhat. These similarities with earlier findings support the observation that general ethnic differences in overall criminal involvement (participation and rate) seem to be maintained even among the more serious offenders in the sample.

Post Arrest Rates by Age

The above findings, along with the earlier findings on age effects, would lead to the expectation that rates of arrest would be lower for cases released at later ages. To investigate this hypothesis, four-year aggregate rates were calculated separately for offenders released from the prison sentences at various ages (the probation groups were not used in this analysis). The results are shown in Table 7.3.

In spite of some variation, resulting in part from the small samples, there was a clear trend for total offense rates to be lower for older releasees among the CDC cases. Sizable peaks can be seen for ages 24 to 25 and for ages 29 to 30, but these peaks do not contradict the general downward trend in

TABLE 7.3 Aggregate yearly arrest rates: Four years postrelease by age at release (all adult prison cases)

Age at release	N	Total	Violent	Violent-economic	Property
20	29	3.36	.47	.26	.80
21	33	2.57	.36	.22	.66
22	70	2.75	.45	.24	1.76
23	93	2.37	.41	.24	.58
24	85	2.70	.68	.41	.61
25	106	3.00	.66	.34	.81
26	74	1.75	.52	.24	.44
27	52	1.90	.48	.23	.40
28	36	1.29	.30	.15	.28
29	32	2.53	.42	.18	1.10
30	23	1.67	.30	.08	.74

these rates. The rates for more specific offense categories showed similar trends for these cases as well.

Pre and Post Arrest Rates by Year

Arrest rates for both total and violent offenses showed similar patterns of escalation for each of the four samples during the four-year period prior to the current sentence. Each of these rates also showed a drop immediately after release, with some continuing decline after that point. The initial levels, rates of escalation, and extent of decline differed among the subsamples, however, resulting in an interesting pattern of differences in rates over time.

The aggregate rates for the four years immediately preceding and following the current sentence are shown in Table 7.4. Also included, for reference, are the rates over the full four-year periods (Pre and Post) and the ratios of the Post rates to the Pre rates.[3] To aid in visualizing the patterns in these rates, they are also displayed graphically in Figures 7.1 and 7.2. Reading down each column of the table, it is clear that for each subsample, the rates for both total offenses and violent offenses showed a marked increase during the four Pre

---

[3] These analyses were not planned initially, and the data set developed for the Pre/post analysis did not include data on individual years prior to the sentence (only four-year and two-year data were calculated). Consequently, the Pre rates in this table were calculated using rates by *age*, with the age at sentencing being considered the first prior year. Obviously, some error will occur, especially for Probation cases, for whom that age may extend into postrelease period as well. As a result, the yearly rates will be inaccurate to some degree and the four-year rates will not, in general, equal the four-year rates in the Table 7.1 (although they are close). The patterns in the data, however, are reasonable, and are unlikely to have resulted merely from these problems in estimation.

TABLE 7.4 Preentry and postrelease arrest rates by year by sample.

Period	CYA/ Probation	CYA/CDC	Suppl./ Probation	Suppl./ CDC	Total
Total Offense Rate					
4th year Pre	2.02	3.78	.82	2.11	2.67
3rd year Pre	2.76	4.25	.87	2.92	3.22
2nd year Pre	2.97	4.84	1.64	4.14	3.96
1st year Pre (sentence)	4.39	7.96	2.55	7.06	5.98
1st year Post	2.21	2.60	1.67	2.32	2.37
2nd year Post	1.36	2.58	.97	2.38	2.08
3rd year Post	1.23	2.58	.80	1.95	1.93
4th year Post	.93	2.23	.73	1.58	1.62
4-year rate (Pre)	3.02	4.94	1.44	3.71	3.34
4-year rate (Post)	1.46	2.52	1.04	2.12	2.04
Ratio (Post/Pre)	.48	.51	.72	.57	.61
Violent Offense Rate					
4th year Pre	.16	.39	.10	.38	.30
3rd year Pre	.10	.46	.22	.43	.36
2nd year Pre	.39	.96	.31	1.22	.83
1st year Pre (sentence)	.72	1.92	.49	2.13	1.40
1st year Post	.33	.52	.35	.62	.49
2nd year Post	.16	.46	.09	.56	.36
3rd year Post	.19	.47	.06	.33	.33
4th year Post	.14	.53	.13	.41	.37
4-year rate (Pre)	.34	.85	.27	.91	.68
4-year rate (Post)	.21	.49	.16	.51	.40
Ratio (Post/Pre).	.62	.58	.59	.56	.59

years, reaching very high levels immediately prior to the current sentence. Part of this increase was caused by including the offenses leading to the current sentence in the Pre-period rates. These "necessarily included" offenses would tend to make rates during this period larger than rates during *any* other period (in which offenders may or may not have had arrests). However, the increase over several years, along with the fact that these rates were very high (up to eight crimes per year), suggests that the "trend" is not simply an artifact of having used these periods in the analysis or of having included the conviction offenses in the calculations.

The initial levels and the rate of increase differed substantially among the subsamples, with the two CDC groups starting higher and reaching a level that was similar to one another and much higher than that of either Probation group. This pattern was especially clear for violent offenses, where the two sets of graphed lines (Figure 7.2) almost coincide. Among the Probation groups, the CYA cases had higher rates for total offenses both initially and at their

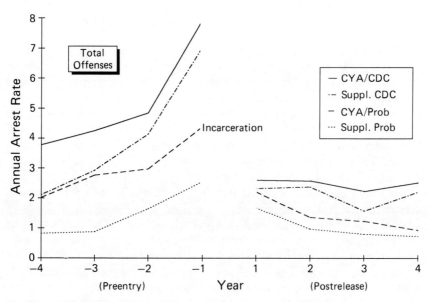

FIGURE 7.1 Aggregate yearly total arrest rates for active offenders, before and after current sentence, by sample.

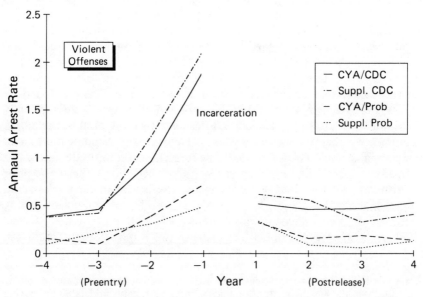

FIGURE 7.2 Aggregate yearly violent arrest rates for active offenders, before and after current sentence, by sample.

peak, but still more similar to the Supplementary Probation cases than to the CDC groups.[4]

While all groups showed a decline in rates of arrest immediately following release (or being placed on probation), that decline was greatest for the two CDC groups, resulting in some convergence in these rates among the four subsamples. It is interesting that the CYA/CDC cases dropped to a level considerably below the level of even four years before their sentences, while the other three groups dropped to levels found in the years more proximate to their sentences. The ratios of four-year Post rates to the four-year Pre rates indicate that each sample showed a considerable overall decrease during the Post period: All but one of these ratios were at or below around .60.

These data strongly suggest that many of these offenders were arrested, convicted, and sent to prison during a period of unusually high levels of criminal behavior: a "crime spree" that was not particularly indicative of their more enduring, personal criminal propensities. Such "spurts" would appear to point once again to the importance of situational factors in the etiology of criminal behavior. Other explanations are possible, however. For example, it is possible that the arrest rate escalation observed during this Pre-incarceration period merely reflects the kind of clustering of arrests that might be observed even if arrests were randomly distributed throughout a "stable" offense career (Maltz and Pollock, 1980; Maltz, Gordon, McDowell, and McCleary, 1980). This "random clustering" would be similar to having a run of, say, four or five "heads" in a row when flipping a coin. Sentences to jail or prison would be more likely during these spurts than at other times during the offenders' careers. From this perspective, we would expect to find such an increase in arrest rates prior to major sentences. Consequently, the spurts themselves would have no particular meaning, and little would be gained by searching for their "causes." However, while some of the increase may be due to this kind of random grouping of crimes and/or arrests, findings reported earlier suggest that differences between arrest rates for various four-year blocks were greater than would be expected if arrests were randomly distributed within stable careers. Closer investigation of this period, to determine whether it is possible to identify factors that precipitate this kind of increase in criminal behavior, should be undertaken in future research.

In any case, these findings suggest that offense behavior in the period prior to prison or probation may be highly uncharacteristic of an offender's overall career, making the use of data from this period problematic for setting sentences or even understanding criminal behavior. For example, Cohen (1986, pg. 323) notes the similarities between two Rand self-report studies in

---

[4] Bear in mind that "probation" sentences also included jail terms for many offenders; for these cases, the sentencing decision may be more reasonably understood as having involved the appropriate *length* of incarceration, rather than simply freedom vs. prison. In California, sentences of up to one year can (and generally are) served in county jail, while longer sentences have to be served in prison.

the distributions of pre-prison offenses, even though the observation "window" periods used in the two studies were different: medians of 28 months and 14 months of street time, respectively. These similarities, which Cohen argues to indicate underreporting in the study with the longer window period, may be due, in large part, to these spurts prior to prison. If most of the crimes are committed immediately prior to prison, the distributions over one versus two years may be, in fact, quite similar, except for particularly high-rate offenses, such as burglary or drug sales (which *were* found to be higher in the study with the longer window period).

The dramatic drop in arrest rates after release from incarceration is very similar to that noted by Murray and Cox (1979) in their study of serious delinquents committed to the Illinois Department of Corrections and of delinquents involved in the Unified Delinquency Intervention Services (UDIS) program. They referred to the mechanism producing this reduction in arrest rates as the "suppression effect." Murray and Cox saw this effect operating primarily through specific deterrence and personal growth of the participants. The deterrent effect came from exposing the delinquents to the reality of institutionalization; the personal growth came as the result of program staffs' taking an interest in the youths. As aids in understanding the similar drop in rates for the present sample, only the deterrence hypothesis seems useful. The realities of adult prison life may well have been made clear to these offenders. It seems unlikely, on the other hand, that these prisoners experienced a great deal of personal growth while in adult prison, since the nature of the intervention is less growth-oriented than the UDIS program. Given the fact that arrest rates during the Pre period were so high, one possible explanation would be that incarceration interrupted the development of whatever situational factors spurred or facilitated the prior escalation in criminal behavior (e.g., a developing drug habit or relationship with a trusted "fence" for stolen goods).

Again, other explanations are possible. If the "random clustering" hypothesis described above were to hold, for example, such a substantial drop in rates would simply be expected, since random processes would tend to bring the criminal behavior of these offenders back to its expected (lower) level (Maltz and Pollock, 1980; Maltz, Gordon, McDowell, and McCleary, 1980). In this view, the rate would be expected to have dropped from the Pre period to the Post period *regardless of what happened to the offender in the interim.* A situational perspective, it should be emphasized, would also predict some drop from these high levels in the absence of any prison sentences, since the circumstances of some offenders would undoubtedly change over time (the kind of instability noted throughout this report). The drop, however, would not be expected to be so great, since no forced disruption of crime-supporting social situations would occur.

It is likely that both of these explanations have some merit. Although it would be interesting to assess their relative strengths, a rigorous test is not likely to be forthcoming. The present data are consistent with both hypotheses and provide no solid basis for deciding between them or for parceling out their respective contributions. Doing so would require determining what would have happened to these arrest rates if the sentences had not been imposed. A rigorous study would thus require that some offenders be allowed to remain free regardless of the number and types of arrests they accumulate (to see if their rates go back down over time, and, if so, how much they decrease). Few would be willing to support such a policy in the name of science.

After the first year back on the street, the total arrest rates for the two CDC groups appeared to stabilize somewhat, while those of Probation groups continued to decline at a moderate rate. These trends served to increase the differences in their rates from that point on.[5] These trends are again consistent with a situational perspective. The differences between prisoners and probationers could be understood, in this view, partly by the degree to which social, situational, or circumstantial factors were carried over from the pre-sentence period into the post-release period. The CDC cases, sentenced to prison for several years, could not as easily return to previous, crime-supporting social situations. While their overall criminal propensities may still have been higher (as evidenced by their maintaining higher rates of arrest even after prison), the situational factors that resulted in the high-rate period prior to prison may thus be expected to change fairly dramatically. The probationers, in contrast, would not have spent very much time incarcerated, and would have found themselves in essentially the same situation as before sentencing.

For violent offenses, similar overall patterns were noted, with the exception that after some initial declines in the Post period, the rates actually showed some increase (the third year for CYA cases and the fourth year for supplementary cases). Similar patterns were found for more specific offenses as well (results not shown). An increase during the fourth year was evident for violent-economic crimes, and rates for property crimes showed an increase during the third year for all except the Supplementary Probation group. Other rates showed some fluctuation, but no trend was evident.

In general, the highest risk for rearrest for these offenders was during the first year on the street after a conviction. The decline over time, though slight, is consistent with earlier findings (Chapter 4) concerning age effects, but it would appear that certain periods (the fourth year for violent-economic crimes, and the third year for property crimes) may run counter to that general tendency.[6]

---

[5] Because of this greater drop after the first year, it is not surprising that studies comparing the postrelease arrest rates of probationers and prisoners over only 24 months have reported small differences (Petersilia and Turner, 1986). While these differences may reflect differences in criminal behavior over the short-run, they should not be used to extrapolate to longer periods of time.

[6] Additional studies (different samples) would help to determine whether these high-risk periods are common to all offenders (rather than peculiar to this sample) and may possibly point to factors that increase the risk during those periods. This kind of information may prove very valuable for understanding situational factors related to criminal behavior and suggest methods for reducing that risk.

Pre and Post Rates by Age

In discussing the rather sharp decrease in rates observed for the Post period as compared to the Pre period for cases sentenced to prison, it was suggested that some decrease in these rates might be expected simply because these individuals aged in prison. The findings on postrelease rates by age lent some credence to this hypothesis, but could not address the issue of whether the Post rates were lower or higher than might be expected simply on the basis of age effects alone. Accordingly, analyses of aggregate arrest rates by age were performed using only the CYA cases who went to adult prison. Arrest rates were calculated for ages prior to their prison sentences and for "active" ages after release (up to, but not including, the age of the last known arrest). Thus, the data for each individual entered into the calculations for those ages prior to his entering prison and for those ages he was active after he was released. The two sets of rates (for total offenses and violent offenses) are shown in Table 7.5 and displayed in Figures 7.3 (total arrests) and 7.4 (violent arrests).

Two clear trends are evident from these data: all rates (except those for Pre violent offenses) declined with increasing age and the post-release rates were lower than the pre-prison rates for all cases at those ages. Note that for the pre-prison rates, the estimates for older ages increasingly refer only to the ages immediately prior to the prison sentences of the cases included, explaining the sharp rise in the total rate for ages 28 and 29 and, to some extent, the wide fluctuations in the rates for violent offenses. Nevertheless, for both total offenses and violent offenses, the arrest rates during the pre-prison period were

TABLE 7.5 Aggregate arrest rates by age for active offenders prior to and following first adult commitment (CYA/CDC cases only).

Age	Preprison active ages			Postprison active ages		
	N	Total	Violent	N	Total	Violent
20	32	4.52	.77	32	5.57	.47
21	60	4.51	.67	60	3.94	.54
22	101	4.34	.86	104	3.18	.41
23	156	4.79	.75	164	2.97	.52
24	158	4.39	.61	191	2.59	.44
25	177	4.15	1.04	237	2.73	.42
26	156	4.14	.72	244	2.19	.33
27	114	3.41	.93	224	2.49	.51
28	90	3.53	.07	197	2.16	.37
29	62	4.00	.50	168	2.01	.25
30				150	2.37	.43
31				125	2.29	.34
32				106	1.79	.36
33				78	1.64	.25
34				46	1.74	.32

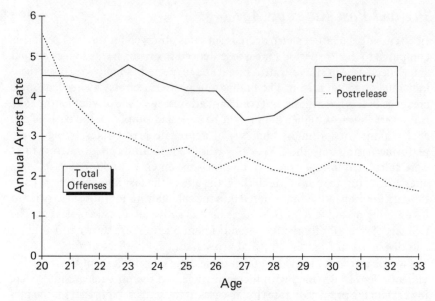

FIGURE 7.3 Aggregate yearly total arrest rates for active offenders by age: Preentry and postrelease (CYA/CDC sample).

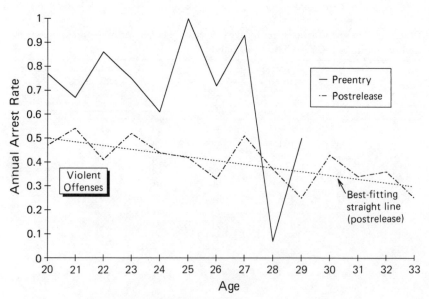

FIGURE 7.4 Aggregate yearly violent arrest rates for active offenders by age: Preentry and postrelease (CYA/CDC sample).

generally higher at each age than were the rates at those ages for offenders released from prison. Postrelease total offense rates showed a sharp decline after age 20, becoming more gradual after age 22 and peaking briefly at ages 27 and 30. The rate for violent offenses showed a less smooth and more gradual decline, again peaking at ages 27 and 30, as well as age 23.

If only the data prior to prison were analyzed, no clear age effect would have been observed for these offenders who went to prison. The preprison escalation in criminal behavior for these offenders, which occurred at various ages, tended to mask the kind of general decline noted for the CYA cohort as a whole (and for these cases as well, when no distinction was made between Pre and Post periods). Thus, because the criminal justice system tends to "select" cases for prison sentences based on having high rates of arrest (and, presumably, of crimes), the cross-sectional study of the preprison behavior of a sample of adult prisoners may be unable to identify important criminal career patterns. The Pre period will simply not provide a very accurate picture of the overall offense behavior of these offenders.

Stability of Pre/Post Arrest Rates

Given the overall decline in rates by age for these cases and the differences between Pre and Post rates, both overall and over time, one would expect stability from Pre to Post to be relatively low. The correlations shown in Table 7.6 reinforce this observation. Shown are the correlations between the rates for the four-year Pre and Post periods, as well as those for the five four-year age-blocks between age 18 and age 37. The Pre/post correlation for total

TABLE 7.6 Arrest-rate correlations: Pre/post and four-year age blocks.

	Pre/ Post	18–21/ 22–25	22–25/ 26–29	26–29/ 30–33	30–33/ 34–37
CDC Cases n =	560	423	329	323	227
Total	.213[a]	.213	.375	.428	.509
Violent	.156	.157	.190	.255	.132
Violent-economic	.169				
Property	.186				
Probation Cases n =	222	274	202	116	45
Total	.386	.446	.324	.251	—[c]
Violent	.140[b]	.013ns	.209	.091ns	—
Violent-economic	.075ns				
Property	.290				

Note: Correlations include cases with at least 12 months of street time for both age blocks. The natural logarithm of all variables was used.
[a] All correlations significant ($p < .01$), unless otherwise noted.
[b] $p < .05$
[c] Too few cases for analysis.

offenses for CDC cases was very low (.213). Note that this correlation (and that for violent offenses as well) is equal to that found between the 18 to 21 age block and the 22 to 25 age block. This similarity is not surprising, considering that the average age at entry to prison was about 22 and the average age at release was around 25; these correlations cover generally the same time periods. As these offenders got older, the correlations between age blocks increased, suggesting that the rates during the post prison periods were more stable, and thereby more indicative of their "true" expected individual arrest rates. Correlations for more specific types of offenses (violent-economic and property offenses) were even lower between Pre and Post. For Probation cases, correlations were similarly low, but were more comparable to the correlation between the 22 to 25 age block and the 26 to 29 age block.

Overall, these correlations indicate that the rates of arrest observable over the Pre period were not very indicative of the relative rates of arrest for these cases during the Post period. This instability is consistent with the notion that many, if not most, of these offenders engaged in uncharacteristic patterns of criminal behavior (including crime sprees) immediately prior to being convicted.

To illustrate the impact of these marginal relationships between Pre and Post rates on the ability to use Pre rates to identify offenders with high Post rates, transitional probabilities from Pre to Post were calculated for cases with

TABLE 7.7 Transitional probabilities for high-rate offenders: Prior to and following prison.

Sample	Number (%)	Post Period		
		Low	Medium	High
Relative Stability				
Total Offenses[a]				
High-rate	185 (33.0%)	41 (22.2%)	70 (37.8%)	74 (40.0%)
Others	375 (67.0%)	131 (34.9%)	134 (35.7%)	110 (29.3%)
Total	560 (100%)	172 (30.7%)	204 (35.6%)	184 (32.9%)
Violent Offenses				
High-rate	176 (31.4%)	67 (38.1%)	39 (22.2%)	70 (39.8%)
Others	384 (68.6%)	207 (53.9%)	67 (17.4%)	110 (28.6%)
Total	560 (100%)	274 (48.9%)	106 (18.9%)	180 (32.1%)
Absolute Stability				
Total Offenses[b]				
High-rate	185 (33.0%)	106 (57.3%)	44 (23.8%)	35 (18.9%)
Others	375 (67.0%)	255 (68.0%)	70 (18.7%)	50 (13.3%)
Total	560 (100%)	361 (64.5%)	114 (20.4%)	85 (15.2%)
Violent Offenses				
High-rate	176 (31.4%)	67 (38.1%)	58 (33.0%)	51 (29.0%)
Others	384 (68.6%)	207 (53.9%)	113 (29.4%)	64 (16.7%)
Total	560 (100%)	274 (48.9%)	171 (30.5%)	115 (20.5%)

[a] All differences statistically significant (Chi-square test) at the .01 level, unless otherwise noted.
[b] $p < .05$.

prison sentences. Of interest were both the *relative stability* of these rates (the extent to which cases with high Pre rates had higher rates in the Post period than other offenders) and the *absolute stability* (the extent to which high-rate offenders maintained those rates during the Post period). The results are shown in Table 7.7.

The top portion of the table shows the percentages of high-rate offenders and non-high-rate offenders with different levels of arrest rates during the Post period, with both sets of rates divided into rough thirds. For both total offenses and violent offenses, less than half (about 45%) of the high-rate cases (Pre) fell into the highest third of cases based on Post rates. Of those cases not identified as high-rate based on pre-prison data, 26.2% had high total rates of arrest and 28.9% had high rates of arrest for violent offenses. Thus, while there was some relationship between the two rate levels, using levels from the Period to predict levels for the Post period would result in over 50% false positive predictions and between 26% and 29% false negative predictions. Further, considerably less than half the high-rate cases during the Post period would have been correctly identified in this manner.

In terms of the proportion of cases maintaining high Pre levels during the Post period, stability is considerably lower because of the overall reduction in rates from Pre to Post. Only 18.9% of the cases with high total rates during the Pre period had rates at the same level during the Post period, compared to 13.3% of those cases that did not have high Pre rates. Stability for violent offenses was somewhat higher, but still less than 30%; in contrast, almost 16% of the cases without high Pre rates had a high arrest rate level for these offenses during the Post period. Again, using Pre rates as the criterion for identifying cases expected to have high rates in the Post period, well over half the high-rate cases would remain unidentified.

Summary

The present data showed that not only did the general trends relative to ethnic differences and age effects hold for the periods prior to and following a major conviction, other trends emerged as well: an escalation of arrest rates prior to conviction and a sharp decrease in these rates following the sentence. These additional trends combined to increase the instability of arrest rates from the Pre period to the Post period over what might have been expected based on earlier analyses of the larger sample. These findings suggest that official data would not be very useful for identifying those offenders who will engage in the highest rates of criminal behavior after release from their current sentences. They also suggest that the period prior to a sentence may be the least useful for studying differences in offense patterns or in offenders. Thus, studies using data referring to the period immediately prior to a prison sentence, such as the major studies conducted by the Rand Corporation (Peterson and Braiker, 1980; Chaiken and Chaiken, 1982; Greenwood, 1982), may be hampered in their ability to isolate patterns that are generally characteristic of criminal careers or to identify important differences among offenders.

Chapter 8
Correlates and Predictors of Arrest Rates for Incarcerated Offenders

The focus of this chapter will be primarily on patterns of association (correlations)[1] between arrest rates and other variables for which data were available: lifestyle variables, such as drug use, marital/family status, and employment; background variables; and variables related to the prison or probation sentences of the offenders in the sample. These analyses were intended primarily to explore the usefulness of these data for understanding differences in arrest rates among those offenders for whom this kind of information was available. Because of the nature of the sample, generalization of the present findings to other offenders is not warranted. Due to the nature of the data, their usefulness even for understanding relationships within this sample are somewhat limited. Before presenting the findings, some discussion of these limitations is in order.

First, recall from Chapter 2 that these data were obtained from prison and probation files. Although prison information was available for virtually all offenders who served prison terms, probation data were available only for offenders with recent exposure to probation. The lifestyle information, then, will not, in general, be indicative of the lifestyles of offenders whose criminal careers ended early and whose levels of criminality were low enough that they avoided sentences to adult prison.

Second, the source of the data and the difficulties encountered in coding them reduce confidence in their validity and reliability. The information was

---

[1] Correlational analysis is not the most appropriate method of studying relationships among all the variables at hand, since most have non-normal distributions and many are dichotomous (coded 0 or 1). Nevertheless, the use of a single measure of association allows for a simple display of the results, so that overall patterns may be more readily apparent. Given the exploratory nature of the present analyses, the reliance on correlational techniques may be excusable. For a more thorough analysis of these associations and/or for the development of a predictive device, other analytic techniques may prove more appropriate.

usually found in narrative form (as part of the "social history") and was often difficult to interpret and code. To the extent possible, all *changes* in drug-use patterns and marital status, as these were noted in the files, were coded. Employment patterns were coded as the number of months employed during calendar years and the most common type of employment during that year. These coded data were then used to establish monthly and yearly indices of drug use, marital status, and employment over the period up to the date of the last available report. As a consequence, the validity and reliability of these data are suspect. Although the split-half correlations for these variables (presented in Chapter 5) indicated reasonable reliability, these correlations were affected by the fact that only those changes noted in the records were coded; uncertainty was coded as stability.

Finally, it is important to note that since information on these variables was taken from official records, they were generally limited to the period up to each offender's final parole or probation report. As a consequence, they often did not extend to the same point as the data on arrests; the rap sheets covered time periods beyond the date of the last report containing lifestyle information. Lifestyle data for later ages must be understood as having been available mostly for offenders still recently active in crime or recently released from prison. In fact, the later the age, the more the sample of cases with available data comes to be comprised of offenders recently or currently engaged in serious crime and/or currently serving major sentences. The data themselves increasingly refer to that period immediately before and/or after a major sentence. Since this time period, as discussed in the last chapter, was exceptional in terms of criminal behavior (increasing criminal behavior, followed by a reduction after release), it would seem likely that the lifestyle indicators during this period would also be exceptional. Data for later ages, therefore, are likely to be increasingly unrepresentative of the age-related lifestyle characteristics of any offenders, inside or outside the sample.

Associations noted for those offenders with available data, however, can be useful for understanding what characteristics tended to go along with differences in arrest rates *for those offenders*. While not generalizable to other offenders, these findings can add to the growing body of data concerning the relationships among these variables for different groups of individuals at different times and under differing conditions.

Using data on indicated changes in drug-use patterns, marital and family status, and periods of employment, percentages of time in which these offenders used various types of drugs, had particular types of family arrangements, and were either employed full-time or unemployed were calculated. These percentages were calculated for the four-year age blocks used previously and for the four-year periods immediately prior to, and following, any incarceration served as part of the probation or prison term. The means, standard deviations, and numbers of cases with available data are shown in Appendix 2 (for the age block analysis) and Appendix 3 (for the

Pre/post analysis).[2] Since the information on lifestyle characteristics was coded for the same four-year age blocks as for the arrest data, correlations between lifestyle variables and arrest rates both within and across age blocks could be calculated. These correlations can provide a basis for understanding how variables relate to arrest rates over time for these offenders. The data for the periods prior to, and following, the incarceration terms can be used to understand these Pre and Post periods as they compare to the arbitrary four-year periods included in the age-block correlations.

The Pre/post information, along with background information and information on the current term, were also included in analyses aimed at the prediction of individual rates of arrest after prison or probation sentences. The intention of these analyses was not to develop a prediction device for identifying high-rate offenders, but rather to understand and illustrate the impact of the criminal career characteristics discussed so far on the ability to predict individual arrest rates. The findings so far would generally lead one to expect only limited success at predicting differences in individual rates of arrest, particularly after a major sentence. On the one hand, arrest rates were shown in Chapter 5 to be fairly *unreliable* as measures of stable individual differences in criminal behavior. On the other hand, arrest rates over time were shown to be relatively *unstable*, so that correlations between one four-year age block and the next were lower than might be expected on the basis of unreliability alone. This instability was found to be particularly high between the period prior to and the period following a sentence to prison or probation. Together, these findings pointed to the limited usefulness of data on prior arrest rates for predicting future rates of arrest and suggested that situational factors play a large part in determining criminal behavior. Under these circumstances, a great deal of success at predicting differences in arrest rates during any particular period using official information on criminal behavior from any other period would not be expected.

Although information on lifestyle characteristics might be expected to provide some additional predictive power, the findings presented in Chapter 5 showed that the increase was marginal when predicting rates during odd or even ages from information on the other half of the career. The explained variance using a regression equation was 59%, compared to the 53% obtained when only arrest rates were used. The behavioral instability present around the time of a major sentence would be expected to reduce this predictive power considerably, so that the accuracy of predicting arrest rates during the post-

---

[2] The percentages for drug use and employment were based on time not incarcerated (street time), while the family status variables referred to total follow-up time (since the individuals presumably retained their family status regardless of incarceration). Unemployment referred to periods in which the offenders had neither employment nor some reason for being unemployed (disabled, enrolled in school, etc.). In the analysis of data for periods prior to, and following, major sentences, employment (the converse of unemployment, as defined above) was used.

release period using available information from prior periods would be expected to be low.

Stability of the Lifestyle Variables

Before turning to the relationships between these variables and arrest rates, it is interesting to note the extent to which these "lifestyle" variables remained stable over time. As with the arrest-rate measures, perfect correlations involving these variables would not be expected even if the underlying behavior were constant, due to the nature of the records on which the coding was based. However, as discussed in Chapter 5, the split-half correlations for these variables were generally higher than for the arrest rates, owing in part to the rules used in coding (patterns were assumed to have continued, unless otherwise noted in the records).

Shown in Table 8.1 are the correlations between adjacent age blocks and between the Pre and Post periods for each of the six lifestyle variables and one additional variable: the percentage of time in each block during which the offender was not incarcerated. Also shown are the means (over each offenders' entire follow-up period) for these lifestyle variables. Again, because of the nature of the coding, these averages cannot be taken as indicators of the "true" extent of these characteristics, but they can serve as rough indications.

As a group, these offenders, most of whom served prison terms as adults,

TABLE 8.1 Age-block and Pre/Post correlations: Lifestyle indicators.

		Correlations				
Variable	Career mean[a]	18–21/ 22–25	22–25/ 26–29	26–29/ 30–33	30–33/ 34–37	Pre/ post percent
% of Street Time						
Heroin use	23.5%	.739[b]	.677	.631	.624	.618
Speed/barbiturates use	21.9%	.720	.741	.571	.542	.577
Hallucinogens use	42.1%	.715	.676	.542	.573	.563
Full-time employment	12.7%	.362	.471	.410	− .016ns	n/a
Unemployed[c]	79.8%	.354	.463	.421	.135[d]	.248
% of All Follow-up						
Not incarcerated	66.0%	.441	.577	.582	.546	.164
Common-law relationship	10.3%	.497	.502	.470	.418	.277
Legally married	10.5%	.462	.541	.571	.430	.275
Supporting dependents	12.0%	.565	.590	.565	.493	n/a

Note: Minimum $n = 201$.
[a] The average of the individual offenders' percentages over their total follow-up periods.
[b] All correlations statistically significant ($p < .01$), unless otherwise noted.
[c] Coded as "percent of time employed" for Pre/post analysis.
[d] $p < .05$.

averaged two-thirds of their time outside incarceration. During that time on the street, the data suggest rather extensive involvement in drug use, with these offenders averaging 23% of their follow-up street time coded as time using heroin and 42% of that time using hallucinogens. While the numbers may not be accurate, they still indicate a considerable extent of drug use among these offenders. Involvement in stable relationships (common-law or marriages), on the other hand, was rather low over the periods covered by these records. On average, these offenders spent only one-fifth of these adult periods involved in these kinds of relationships. The percentage of time during which they contributed to the support of dependents was slightly higher, indicating that some offenders continued to support dependent children after relationships ended. The average percentage of time unemployed (no noted employment) was high for this sample, averaging 80%, with full-time employment accounting for slightly over half the time spent employed. Taken together, the low averages for family involvement and employment suggest that these offenders tended to maintain, at best, marginal linkages to dominant social institutions during these years.

The correlations between adjacent age-block variables reveal as much about how the variables were coded as they do about the stability of the characteristic in question. In fact, given that statuses were considered stable unless otherwise noted, there is more instability indicated than might be expected. For example, the highest correlations across age blocks were found for drug use during the ages of 18 to 29; the fact that these correlations were only around .70 indicates that some changes in drug-use patterns were noted in the records. Other variables were correlated at about the same level as was found for total arrest rates: around .40 to .50. For most variables, the correlations for all adjacent age blocks and for the Pre/post variables were similar. For marital status variables, however, the Pre/post correlations were considerably lower, suggesting greater instability during that period with respect to marriages or common-law relationships. Percent of time on the street was least stable from Pre-incarceration to Post-incarceration.

Age-Block Correlations

Correlations between lifestyle variables and arrest rates (total offenses and violent offenses) were calculated for all cases and for CDC cases separately. Also included were selected background variables and a variable indicating whether the offender had an adult prison term. From these correlations, a picture of how these variables related to one another over time could be gained. The correlation matrices were reviewed to identify patterns of association and differences for offense types (total vs. violent) and for samples (all cases vs. CDC cases only). The results of these analyses will be discussed in general terms, with the actual correlations presented only for the analysis involving all cases and total offenses.

In reviewing the four sets of correlations, several general patterns emerged. First, except for the variables indicating the percentage of time during each block in which the offenders were not incarcerated, all the correlations were fairly low. Second, concurrent relationships (within-block correlations) were greater than predictive ones, with only a few exceptions. Third, the correlations were highest when all cases were included in the analysis; separate analyses using only those cases with adult prison sentences (CDC cases) resulted in similar patterns, with all correlations lower than for all cases combined. Fourth, correlations involving rates of arrest for violent offenses were generally lower than those involving rates for total offenses; a few interesting differences were observed, however.

Table 8.2 shows the statistically significant (nonzero) correlations between total rates of arrest and the major lifestyle variables for the five age blocks. The highest correlations were between percentages of time on the street during these age blocks and the rates of arrest. These correlations were all negative, indicating that those offenders with the highest rates of arrest tended to spend

TABLE 8.2 Correlations with total arrest rates for age blocks: All cases with prison or probation information.

	Arrest rate (total offenses)				
	18–21	22–25	26–29	30–33	34–37
% Street Time					
18–21	−.5584[a]	−.1810[a]	−.1411[a]	—	—
22–25	−.3391[a]	−.5128[a]	−.1481[a]	—	—
26–29	−.1404[a]	−.3539[a]	−.4276[a]	−.1643[a]	—
30–33	—	−.2281[a]	−.4233[a]	−.5328[a]	−.2731[a]
34–37	—	—	−.1387[a]	−.3654[a]	−.4989[a]
% Time: Heroin Use					
18–21	.2144[a]	.2996[a]	.1576[a]	.1192[a]	—
22–25	.1760[a]	.3616[a]	.3115[a]	.1884[a]	—
26–29	.1134[a]	.2448[a]	.2656[a]	.2686[a]	.2930[a]
30–33	—	.1184[b]	.0923[b]	.2268[a]	.3190[a]
34–37	—	.1601[b]	—	—	.2775[a]
% Time: Uppers/Downers Use					
18–21	.1805[a]	.1782[a]	.0661[b]	.1145[a]	—
22–25	.1729[a]	.2242[a]	.1267[a]	.1672[a]	—
26–29	.0965[a]	.1563[a]	.1742[a]	.1877[a]	—
30–33	—	.1205[a]	.1016[b]	.2757[a]	.1221[b]
34–37	—	.1316[b]	—	.1511[a]	.1312[b]
% Time: Hallucinogens Use					
18–21	.2025[a]	.1804[a]	.0843[b]	.0789[b]	—
22–25	.2016[a]	.2865[a]	.2022[a]	.0972[b]	.1189[b]
26–29	.0791[b]	.1599[a]	.2690[a]	.2011[a]	.2263[a]
30–33	—	.0920[b]	—	.2440[a]	.3254[a]
34–37	—	—	—	.1204[b]	.3880[a]

TABLE 8.2 (*Contd.*)

	Arrest rate (total offenses)				
	18–21	22–25	26–29	30–33	34–37
% Time: Common-law					
18–21	.0877[a]	.0692[b]	—	—	—
22–25	.0986[a]	.1508[a]	.0980[a]	.1182[a]	.1136[b]
26–29	—	.1137[a]	.1223[a]	.1166[a]	.1793[a]
30–33	—	—	—	.1270[a]	.1119[b]
34–37	—	—	—	—	.2847[a]
% Time: Legally Married					
18–21	− .0840[a]	—	—	—	—
22–25	—	—	.0845[b]	—	—
26–29	—	—	.1162[a]	—	—
30–33	—	—	—	.0919[b]	—
34–37	—		.0925[b]	.1337[a]	.1764[a]
% Time: Supporting Dependents					
18–21	—	—	.0897[b]	—	—
22–25	—	—	.1065[a]	—	—
26–29	—	—	.0983[a]	.1007[b]	.1256[b]
30–33	—	—	—	.1097[a]	.1926[a]
34–37	—	—	—	—	.2204[a]
% Time: Employed Full-time					
18–21	− .0770[b]	—	− .1094[a]	—	—
22–25	− .1029[a]	− .0766[b]	− .0906[b]	—	—
26–29	− .1070[a]	—	—	—	—
30–33	− .1294[a]	—	—	—	—
34–37	—	—	—	—	—
% Time: Unemployed					
18–21	—	—	—	—	—
22–25	—	—	—	—	—
26–29	—	—	− .1523[a]	—	—
30–33	—	—	—	− .1104[a]	—
34–37	—	—	—	—	− .1024[b]
Background Information					
Criminality:					
Father	.0809[a]	.1084[a]	—	—	—
Siblings	.1662[a]	.2053[a]	.1503[a]	—	—
Age at first:					
Arrest	− .4270[a]	− .2664[a]	− .1377[a]	—	—
Commitment	− .4159[a]	− .2305[a]	− .1368[a]	—	—
No. escapes	.1731[a]	—	—	—	—
Claimed school grade	—	− .1243[a]	—	—	—
Adult prison	.3539[a]	.3729[a]	.2265[a]	.1678[a]	—

Note: The natural logarithms of the arrest rate variables were used.

[a] $p < .01$.

[b] $p < .05$.

the largest portions of these periods behind bars. It is noteworthy that the correlations between rates of arrest in each age block and percentages of street time in the next block were considerably higher than between these rates and percentages of street time in *preceding* blocks. This pattern indicates that incarceration time did not precede higher arrest rates to the same extent that arrest rates led to greater incarceration time.

Drug Use

The next highest correlations were positive and indicated that, among the variables included in the analysis, differences in drug use were the most closely linked to differences in the rates of arrest. Still, these correlations were not particularly high, the highest being for heroin use within the 22 to 25-year-old age block. After age 25, predictive relationships for heroin use were slightly stronger than concurrent ones; this was the only variable for which this predictive pattern was found.

The use of other drugs—amphetemines and barbiturates ("uppers and downers") and hallucinogenic drugs—was also related to arrest rates, but, again, not strongly. Correlations for these forms of drug use were highest within age blocks, becoming smaller and smaller as the time difference between the two age blocks increased. These patterns may suggest that drug use and criminal behavior are merely *associated* (the highest rates of arrest occur while the individual is using drugs) and that any cross-block correlations result merely from the fact that both drug use and criminal behavior have some modicum of stability over time. However, the relationship between the use of these drugs and subsequent arrest rates was stronger, in general, than between arrest rates and subsequent drug use. This pattern appears to indicate a possible causal relationship; drug use in one period leads to higher rates of arrest later on. Still, the fact that the differences in these correlations were not great would indicate that any causal relationship is not a particularly strong one.

Marital/Family Status

The correlations for the family status variables indicate that, contrary to common assumptions, this sample of offenders did not benefit from the common-law or legal marriages (however fleeting) in their lives, at least in terms of their being arrested. Except for the single negative relationship between time spent legally married and arrest rates during the 18 to 21 age block, all the statistically significant correlations involving common-law relationships, marriage, or the support of dependents were positive. While no attempt was made to investigate the possible bases for such a curious finding, one possible explanation may be that these relationships impose an increased financial burden on the individual. Those unable or unwilling to meet this obligation through legitimate employment may turn to crime as a way of making money. Whatever the reason, the data suggest that the normal settling effect of family relationships did not occur for these offenders.

Employment

The correlations between arrest rates and the extent of full-time employment were in the expected direction (more full-time employment associated with lower rates of arrest) and point to the reciprocal influence of these factors. Reading across the top two lines, these statistically significant correlations suggest that full-time employment during the early twenties (18–25) was related to lower rates of arrest not only during those age blocks but also in later age blocks (26–29). On the other side of the coin, reading down the first column, the correlations indicate that higher rates of arrest during the 18 to 21 age block were related to lower amounts of full-time employment in each subsequent age block up to age 33.

The only significant correlations between unemployment and arrest rates were found for later age blocks. These negative relationships indicate that, for these offenders, the greater the percentage of time during which there was no documented employment, school, or disability in these periods, the lower the rate of arrest. Although no ready explanation for this curious relationship is offered, a review of the correlations among the lifestyle variables suggests a possible clue: positive relationships among drug use, family involvement, and employment, especially during older age blocks. A positive correlation between family involvement and employment would be expected, but the fact that increases in drug use were associated with increases in family involvement and employment is not so easy to understand. It could be that increases in drug use lead to increased financial need, which, in turn, may have led either to increased employment or increased criminal behavior (or both). Family involvement, as suggested earlier, may have had a similar effect on financial need. Of course, no simple explanation is likely to suffice, since financial considerations cannot completely explain the relationship between drug use and criminal behavior and are not likely to explain the relationship between family involvement and drug use. There are obviously a number of factors involved in creating these interrelationships, and a more detailed study of these patterns is called for.

Background Characteristics

These correlations indicate that higher arrest rates were related to having other family members with criminal histories and to the age at which the offender was first arrested or first committed to a lock-up facility. Familial criminality was most strongly related to arrest rates during the 22 to 25 age block, while the age at first arrest was most strongly related to the 18 to 21 arrest rates. Of course, these relationships have been observed before; of interest in the present instance is that these relationships decreased over time, falling to zero after age 29. In fact, from age 30 on, none of these background variables was correlated with rates of arrest for these offenders. This pattern indicates that these kinds of background variables no longer served to differentiate among those offenders who remained seriously active in crime after the age of 30.

Violent Offenses Only

As mentioned earlier, the correlations of these lifestyle and background variables with rates of arrest for violent offenses were generally smaller than for all offenses combined. Correlations with lifestyle variables followed similar patterns as for total arrests, with fewer correlations reaching statistical significance. However, there were some differences in the correlations involving background variables than were found for total arrest rates. While correlations involving sibling criminality and age at first arrest (or commitment) were somewhat smaller, statistically significant relationships were found for some variables not present when total arrest rates were used. Among these variables were family instability (indicated by whether the family was intact), which was correlated with early rates of violent arrests; whether or not the family obtained welfare payments; known criminality on the part of the father or mother; and serious criminality on the part of siblings (prison or jail sentences). All these variables indicate the existence of unstable or unhealthy family environments. Whether or not these differences indicate possible differences in the etiology of violent criminality (over general criminality) is uncertain, but deserves closer study in the future.

In general, while there was some tendency for statuses and rates to vary together, the relationships were not strong, at least not strong enough to suggest a great deal of predictive value for information on drug use, employment, or family status.

Pre/Post Correlations

These analyses focused on correlations with arrest rates observed over the four-year period after release from jail or prison. In addition to the lifestyle and background variables included above, this analysis also included variables related to the current term and variables specific to offenders convicted of robbery or burglary, since these cases were of primary interest in the Rand study on selective incapacitation (Greenwood, 1982). One of these variables, the "Rand Score," was created so as to be as close as possible to the scale developed by Greenwood for identifying high-rate offenders among incoming California prisoners. It was created (for robbers and burglars only) by giving a score of "1" for each of the following characteristics (zero otherwise) and summing them for each offender:

1—Prior conviction for the instant offense (robbery of burglary).
2—Incarcerated for more than 50% of the preceding two years.
3—Known arrest prior to age 16.
4—State-level juvenile commitment.
5—Any drug use in the preceding two years.
6—Any juvenile drug use.
7—Employed less than 50% of the preceding two years.

Notably absent from this seven-point scale is any direct reference to the offender's criminal behavior during the Pre-prison period. The Rand study did not have follow-up data on their sample of prisoners, and Greenwood was therefore forced to establish his predictive scale using concurrent (prior)

TABLE 8.3 Correlations with Post arrest rates: All cases with prison or probation information.

	Arrest rate (Post)				
	Total	Violent	Violent-economic	Property	Street time %
Arrest Rate (Post)					
Total					−.5866[a]
Violent	.5551[a]				−.4314[a]
Violent-economic	.4510[a]	.8109[a]			−.4223[a]
Property	.6624[a]	.1569[a]	.1560[a]		−.4494[a]
Arrest Rate (Pre)					
Total	.3463[a]	.2246[a]	.1805[a]	.1885[a]	−.2604[a]
Violent	.0842[a]	.2080[a]	.1719[a]	—	−.1276[a]
Violent-economic	—	.1666[a]	.2047[a]	—	−.0759[b]
Property	.1881[a]	.1085[a]	.0800[b]	.2471[a]	−.1882[a]
% of Time (Pre)					
Heroin use	.1888[a]	—	.0795[b]	.1240[a]	−.1440[a]
Uppers/downers use	.1197[a]	.0794[b]	.0979[a]	.1239[a]	−.1323[a]
Hallucinogens use	.0777[b]	—	.0609[b]	—	—
Common-law relationship	—	—	—	—	—
Legally married	—	—	—	—	—
Employed	−.0910[a]	—	—	−.1119[a]	.0923[a]
Not incarc. (street time)	−.1595[a]	−.1704[a]	−.1033[a]	−.0726[b]	.1643[a]
% of Time (Post)					
Heroin use	.3061[a]	.1422[a]	.1595[a]	.1960[a]	−.2166[a]
Uppers/downers use	.1520[a]	.1052[a]	.1162[a]	.1151[a]	−.1684[a]
Hallucinogens use	.2259[a]	.1783[a]	.1640[a]	.1332[a]	−.1952[a]
Common-law relationship	.1045[a]	—	.0597[b]	.0638[b]	—
Legally married	.1086[a]	—	—	.0613[b]	−.0548[b]
Employed	−.2834[a]	−.1889[a]	−.1802[a]	−.1629[a]	.3119[a]

TABLE 8.3 (*Contd.*)

	Arrest rate (Post)				
	Total	Violent	Violent-economic	Property	Street time %
Race					
White	− .0760[b]	− .1433[b]	− .1232[a]	—	—
Black	.0575[b]	.1501[a]	.1294[a]	—	− .0580[b]
Hispanic	—	—	—	—	—
Background Information					
Number of siblings	− .0768[b]	—	—	—	—
Known welfare recipient	—	.1414[a]	.1252[a]	—	− .0787[b]
Intact family	—	− .0579[b]	—	—	—
Any criminality (father)	.1113[a]	.1469[a]	.1382[a]	.0842[a]	− .0964[a]
Any criminality (mother)	—	.0728[b]	—	—	− .0793[b]
Any criminality (siblings)	.1140[b]	.0850[a]	.0906[a]	.0984[a]	− .1336[a]
Age at first arrest	− .1809[a]	− .1157[a]	− .1106[a]	− .1077[a]	.1270[a]
Age at first commitment	− .1622[a]	− .0772[b]	− .0715[b]	− .0913[a]	—
Number of prior escapes	—	—	—	—	− .0587[b]
Number of drugs as juvenile	.1944[a]	.1125[a]	.1062[a]	.0802[b]	− .1297[a]
Any juvenile drug use	.1848[a]	.0898[a]	.0903[a]	.0787[b]	− .1147[a]
Commitment Offense					
Includes Robbery	− .0634[b]	.0714[b]	.1324[a]	− .0722[b]	—
Includes Burglary	—	—	− .0740[b]	.1027[a]	—
Number of crimes	—	− .0594[b]	—	—	—
Prior Conviction					
For Robbery	—	.0638[b]	—	—	—
For Burglary	—	—	.0695[b]	.1232[a]	− .1097[a]
Rand Score					
Robbers (*n* = 233)	—	.1509[b]	.1223[b]	—	—
Burglars (*n* = 272)	.2547[a]	.1643[a]	.1142[b]	.2005[a]	− .2400[a]
Current Term (CDC)					
Age at entry	− .0817[b]	− .1086[a]	− .1216[a]	—	.1509[a]
Age at release	− .2303[a]	—	− .0819[b]	− .1221[a]	.2187[b]
Length of stay	− .2185[a]	—	—	− .1614[a]	.0987[a]
Juvenile commitment (CYA)	—	—	—	—	.2045[a]
Drug/alochol treatment	.1476[a]	—	.0920[b]	—	− .1521[a]
Medication treatment	—	.0735[b]	—	—	—
Vocational training	—	—	—	—	.0850[b]
No. of disciplinaries	.1126[a]	.1679[a]	.1342[a]	—	− .1474[a]
Serious disciplinary	—	.1882[a]	.1373[a]	—	− .0989[a]
Known enemies	.0900[b]	.1426[a]	.0918[b]	—	− .0879[b]
Known gang affiliation	—	.0892[b]	—	—	− .0778[b]
Parole or Probation (All Cases)					
Drug treatment, testing	.1622[a]	—	—	.0936[a]	—

[a] $P < .01$

[b] $P < .05$

offense data. Since the offense rates for these offenders were assumed to be relatively stable, such a procedure was deemed justified, although Greenwood recognized the need for prospective validation of the predictive power of the scale. A prospective study would undoubtedly have included prior criminal behavior among the predictor variables.

The nonzero (statistically significant) correlations are shown in Table 8.3. As before, only those correlations involving all cases (those with prison terms and those with probation terms) are presented. Some variables referred specifically to prison terms; these correlations included only those cases with prison terms. Findings for separate analyses in which only the cases with prison terms were included will be referred to at times in the discussion.

In general, these Pre/post correlations, like the age-block correlations, were generally low. Those correlations involving arrest rates for total offenses were typically higher than those involving more specific kinds of offenses. The highest correlations, other than those among the Post-period arrest rates, were with prior rates of arrest. For violent-economic and property offenses, the highest correlations involved these specific rates during the Pre period, although Pre total arrest rates were nearly as high. Prior rates of arrest for violent-economic crimes were not related to subsequent total arrest rates or to subsequent rates of arrest for property crimes.

Lifestyle Variables

Lifestyle variables during the Pre period were not highly correlated with Post arrest rates in this sample. In separate analyses, involving only those cases with adult prison terms, most of these correlations dropped to zero. The main Pre-period lifestyle variables significantly related to Post-period arrest rates were heroin use (with total arrest rate) and uppers/downers use (with property arrest rate). Thus, while the lifestyle variables had some predictive usefulness within the broader sample, they could not aid in differentiating among the more serious offenders who received prison sentences.

Concurrent associations, on the other hand, generally held for both the combined sample and for prison (CDC) cases alone. These correlations, except for the employment variable, however, were smaller than those found within age blocks. The correlation with percentage of time employed, in fact, ran counter to the earlier finding of either no relationship or a positive one (more employment/higher arrest rates). For both the total sample and CDC cases separately, the negative correlations indicate that more employment during the Post period was associated with a lower arrest-rate level during that period. Further investigation of these data, to reconcile the apparent inconsistency between these correlations and those found earlier, are certainly in order. In the meantime, it would appear that efforts to increase the employment of individuals placed on probation or parole have some merit, if only over the short run.

Ethnicity and Background Variables

Correlations with ethnicity variables and background variables were consistent with earlier findings. Blacks showed higher rates of total, violent, and violent-economic crimes, but did not differ from others with respect to property crimes. Fathers' and siblings' criminality and the age at first arrest (or commitment) were found to be related to rates of all types of crimes in the Post period. Also related to all types of crime were indicators of juvenile drug use; the number of different drugs was slightly more predictive than whether or not the record indicated any drug use as a juvenile. Indicators of family instability, poverty, and maternal criminality were related to rates of violent crimes only.

Robbery or Burglary

Correlations focusing on robbery and burglary showed that those offenders committed for robbery had higher rates of arrest for related crimes (violent and violent-economic) and lower rates for total crimes and property crimes. Burglars showed the opposite tendency (lower violent-economic rates and higher property rates.) These patterns indicate some tendency of these offenders to specialize, relative to other offenders. Prior convictions for robbery (among all offenders) showed little relationship to Post rates of crimes, while prior convictions for burglary had a relatively strong association with Post property arrest rates and a lesser (but significant) relationship with rates of violent-economic crimes. This latter association suggests that in addition to their tendency to continue committing property crimes, burglars also have the potential for violence in the context of their economically oriented criminal behavior. Correlations involving the Rand Scores were, at best, moderate, compared to other variables. High correlations for these variables would not be expected, since the scale did not include prior criminal behavior.

Current Term Information

Few variables related to the current sentence were available for probationers, and the few that were available (age at sentence, age at release from jail, whether a jail term was included in the sentence, and the length of stay in jail) were unrelated to any of the outcome measures. More information was available from prison files, however, and some variables proved to be associated with outcome.

Age at entry, age at release, and length of stay were all negatively associated with some or all of the Post arrest rates, and all were related to the percentage of time during the Post four-year period in which the offenders were not incarcerated. Post arrest rates did not differ for those cases with prior commitments to the California Youth Authority; those offenders did, however, manage to spend higher proportions of the follow-up period on the street. This latter finding appears to contradict those of the Rand study (Greenwood, 1982), in which state-level juvenile commitments were found to be predictive of rates of criminal behavior.[3]

Also related to Post-period arrest rates were the number of disciplinary infractions accumulated during the prison term, the presence of serious disciplinary infractions, any indication of the offender's having enemies among the other inmates, and any indication of gang membership in prison. All these variables were related primarily to rates of violent arrests during the Post period. It is likely that these variables serve primarily as indicators of existing criminal propensity among prisoners (rather than as indicating a causal link between behavior and social arrangements in prison and subsequent behavior), since they tend to be even more highly correlated with rates of arrest during the Pre period. A notable exception is the variables indicating "known enemies" in prison. This variable was uncorrelated with Pre arrest rates, suggesting that conflicts within prison may have a direct affect on criminal behavior (especially violence) after release.

Not included in the tables (and uncorrelated with rates of Post-period arrests) were variables indicating levels of academic achievement, self-reported school grade level, IQ, and whether or not the offender received vocational or educational training while incarcerated. A variable indicating drug/alcohol treatment was related to arrest rates for total offenses and violent-economic offenses, suggesting that those cases deemed in need of such treatment were, in fact, more criminally inclined, but the data do not allow for an assessment of any possible effect the treatment may have had on subsequent criminal behavior.

Prediction of Postrelease Arrest Rates

Multiple regression techniques were used to explore the usefulness of the above variables for developing a scale that would predict arrest rates during the post-release period. The sample was divided in half, with each half serving as a separate construction sample and as a cross-validation sample for the other half. Total and violent arrest rates (logged) were regressed, stepwise, on most of the variables included in Table 8.3.

Results for the total sample and for CDC cases separately were similar, in terms of the kinds of variables involved. Prediction accuracy, in both the

---

[3] On further investigation, it was found that former CYA cases did have higher rates of arrest (total offenses) during the *Pre* period. Since Greenwood's offense data were only for the Pre period, these data are consistent with them in that regard. Not readily apparent is why these cases would differ in their rates of arrest during the Pre period only, unless the prison terms had a different impact on the CYA cases than on those with no CYA history.

construction and validation samples, was somewhat higher for the total sample, as would be expected on the basis of the higher correlations. The regression equations accounted for around 17% of the variance in Post arrest rates (total offenses) within the two randomly selected half-samples (Multiple R^2 values were .158 and .180) and around 12% of the variance in these rates when each was applied to the other half of the sample (cross-validation). For CDC cases only, Multiple R^2 values within samples dropped to around .096 (9.6% of the variance accounted for). Multiple R^2 values found when the two equations were applied to the other half of the sample of CDC cases dropped to around .040 (4% of the variance in arrest rates). Thus, the regression analyses did not produce very powerful prediction equations, even when both Prior information and institutional information were included.

The prediction equations for the two random half-samples did not include exactly the same variables; only the Prior rate of arrest for all offenses entered both equations. In part, this difference was caused by the shear number of variables available for inclusion, many of which were somewhat overlapping or redundant. Thus, when the "types" of variables included in these equations were considered, more similarity was evident. Common "types" of predictor variables, among those referring to the Prior period or the incarceration term, included prior drug use, low prior violence, and institutional enemies or gang affiliation. These commonalities were found for those analyses limited to CDC cases in these two half-samples, as well.

For the total sample, no other common variables entered the equations. In one half of the sample, age at release, parole/probation employment (offenders who were "mostly employed" had lower rates of arrest), and father's criminality entered after the Prior and Incarceration-term variables. In the other half, a variable indicating parole/probation drug treatment entered (with treated offenders showing higher rates) and ethnic and sample differences were found; after controlling for other variables, blacks were found to have higher average Post arrest rates, and lower rates were found for those in the Supplementary Probation sample.

Age at release entered both equations for the CDC cases only. Beyond this one additional common variable, no other common variables were found. One equation included parole employment and father's criminality, while the other equation included only ethnicity (whites had lower Post rates, on average, in this subsample). The amount of variance explained by the equations increased only slightly with the addition of these variables.

The usefulness of these equations for predicting arrest-rate levels during the Post period was explored by changing the "common variables" into variables indicating particular traits. These variables (coded 0, 1) were then summed to create a scale score for *Prior Factors*, a scale score for *Institutional Factors*, and a score for *All Factors* combined. Since the institutional factors relate primarily to cases with adult prison terms, this analysis was performed for CDC cases only. The percentages of those cases with low, medium, or high rates of arrest during the Post period who had each particular trait and the percentages who scored at various levels on the prediction scales are shown in Table 8.4. It is apparent from these figures that none of the traits was strongly related to differences in levels of Post arrest rates. Further, the scale scores derived from these traits had only moderate (though statistically significant) relationships to these arrest-rate levels.

Among the Prior factors, having an arrest rate over 5.5 per year (the top third of the distribution for these offenders) was the strongest predictor of

TABLE 8.4 Percentages of postprison arrest-rate groups[a] with risk-score traits and scale-score levels.

	Post-period arrest rate			
Variable	Low (n = 180)	Medium (n = 218)	High (n = 196)	Total (n = 594)
Risk Factors (Prior Period)				
Prior rate (total) > 5.5	23.3%	33.8%	40.2%	33.2%
Prior heroin use (any)	30.5%	45.0%	51.6%	42.6%
Juvenile: Heroin use	18.3%	25.2%	28.1%	23.1%
Juvenile: 3 + Drugs used	27.8%	35.3%	36.2%	32.1%
Risk Factors (Institutional Stay)				
Length of stay < 36 mos.	52.2%	62.8%	71.4%	60.7%
Age at release < 24	30.6%	38.5%	44.9%	34.6%
Drug treatment this term	36.6%	49.6%	57.4%	47.9%
Disciplinaries this term > 4	34.5%	39.0%	47.3%	40.9%
Major disciplinary this term	18.3%	24.3%	24.0%	24.3%
Known enemies in prison	11.1%	18.3%	21.9%	17.3%
Risk Score (Prior Factors)[b]	(n = 171)	(n = 204)	(n = 183)	(n = 558)
Low 0 (n = 178)	43.9%	28.9%	24.0%	31.9%
Medium 1 (n = 177)	30.4%	31.9%	32.8%	31.7%
High 2 + (n = 203)	25.7%	39.2%	43.2%	36.4%
Mean Score (Prior Factors)[c]	.99	1.39	1.59	1.33
Risk Score (Institutional Factors)[b]	(n = 107)	(n = 123)	(n = 120)	(n = 350)
Low 0–1 (n = 82)	38.3%	21.1%	12.5%	23.4%
Medium 2 (n = 112)	37.4%	32.5%	26.7%	32.0%
High 3 + (n = 156)	24.3%	46.3%	60.8%	44.6%
Mean score (Inst. factors)[3]	1.85	2.37	2.68	2.32
Risk Score (All Factors)[b]	(n = 103)	(n = 115)	(n = 112)	(n = 330)
Low 0–2 (n = 101)	46.6%	27.8%	18.8%	30.6%
Medium 3–4 (n = 124)	30.1%	40.9%	41.1%	37.6%
High 5 + (n = 105)	23.3%	31.3%	40.2%	31.8%
Mean Score (All Factors)[c]	2.94	3.77	4.17	3.65

Note: The percentages for the risk scale score levels may not add to 100, due to rounding.

[a] Only those cases with adult prison terms were included.
[b] $p < .01$ (Chi-square test).
[c] $p < .01$ (Analysis of variance).

having a high arrest rate in the Post period; in fact, this trait alone had almost as much predictive power as did being in the top third of the distribution on the Risk-scale score containing all Prior factors. In all, 43.2% of those with high rates of arrest during the Post period had two or more of these Prior risk-factor traits. Conversely, of the 203 cases with two or more traits, 21.7% had low Post arrest rates, 39.4% had medium rates of arrest, and 38.9% had high rates (these figures are not shown in the table). Thus, the Prior period factors were not able to pick out the high-rate offenders very well; only 38% of those predicted on the basis of Presentence information to be high-rate offenders in the Post period actually were. The others (almost 62%) were false positives. This level of prediction accuracy certainly would not serve the purposes of a risk-based policy of selective incapacitation.

The factors related to the institutional terms of these offenders were somewhat more predictive of differences in Post-period rates, but less than half the sample had valid data for all six variables. While none of the individual factors appeared strongly related to Post arrest-rate levels, the total risk score showed sharper distinctions for arrest-rate groups than did the score based on Prior factors. Of those with high Post arrest rates, 12.5% scored low on this six-point scale, while 60.8% scored high; in contrast, 38.3% of the low-arrest-rate group scored low on this scale, while only 24.3% scored high. Calculating the percentages in the other direction, results indicate that of the 156 with high scores on this small scale, only 16.7% had low Post arrest rates, while 46.8% had high rates of arrest after release. Evidently, for these offenders, information related to their terms of imprisonment was more useful for predicting their postrelease behavior than information about earlier periods of time.

When the two sets of factors were combined, some predictive power was actually lost. The two sets of factors combined to create a scale with slightly lower predictive power than the scale based on institutional factors alone, although this combined scale was better than the Prior factors by themselves.

Again, the present scales were derived in rather rough fashion from the results of similarly rough regression analyses. A more careful and thorough-going analysis of these data may be able to improve on these prediction scales. However, as argued throughout, by the nature of both criminal behavior itself and the current measure of it (arrests), little success at identifying those individuals with the highest Post-release rates of criminal behavior would be expected. The unreliability of the measures and the instability of the behaviour combined to introduce a considerable amount of unexplainable variation in the arrest rates of these offenders— unexplainable, at least, in terms of the variables on hand. Thus, while it is possible that the "right" predictors were simply not available here, and that some future study *may* discover the combination of variables that allows for reasonably accurate prediction of future offense (or arrest) rates, a great deal more success at predicting this unstable behavior (at its most unstable point) using unstable predictors, all of which are indicated by relatively unreliable measures, would not be expected.

Summary

Consistent with expectations, the analyses described above all point to the difficulty of predicting differences in arrest rates, especially during the period after release from incarceration. Most relationships were found to be strongest *during* particular periods of time, while "predictive" relationships (correlations between arrest rates in one period and other variables in *prior* periods) were much weaker. When only those cases with adult prison sentences were considered, strong relationships were even harder to find, indicating that the more serious offenders were less easily differentiated *from one another* than they were from the less serious offenders with probation sentences. Regression analyses were only marginally successful at selecting combinations of variables that predicted postsentence rates of arrest. These findings point once again to the difficulty of successfully identifying the offenders who will have the highest levels of criminality after a particular sentence is served and, consequently, to the difficulty in developing an efficient policy of selective incapacitation based on prediction of risk.

Chapter 9
Incapacitation Effects of Increased Prison Terms

Laws and policies regarding whether or not to sentence particular offenders to prison and how long they should serve are based, in part, on the believed "effects" of incarceration. Included among these effects are punishment (or "just deserts"), the possibility that the offender (and others) will be deterred from committing crimes in the future, and the possibility that the offender might be rehabilitated by the programs offered in prison. Added to these reasons for incarcerating offenders is the fact that offenders who are sentenced to prison are prevented from committing crimes in the wider society for the duration of their incarceration. Uncertainty as to whether prison has any sizable deterrent or rehabilitative effects has led many people to believe that only through incapacitating offenders can prison have any major effect on overall levels of crime. If the offenders subjected to prison sentences can be expected to commit crimes at very high rates while on the street *and* if those crimes would not be committed by someone else in their absence, such policies could have a profound impact on levels of crime in society. If prison is viewed from this perspective, a major issue is how to maximize the crime-reduction benefit of prison while minimizing its cost. Proponents of selective incapacitation argue that by adjusting sentence lengths on the basis of the number of crimes different offenders can be expected to commit when they are released, a larger crime-reduction effect could be achieved with the same amount of prison space. Selective sentencing policies are seen as a way of increasing the number of crimes prevented per person-year of prison use.

The data presented so far, however, have all pointed to a great deal of instability in criminal careers and have thereby called into question both the practicality of selective sentencing policies and the adequacy of current methods of estimating incapacitative effects. Still, these findings do not invalidate the notion that, since some offenders can be expected to commit crimes at higher rates than others, some reduction of crime in society (or some increase in prison efficiency) could be realized by a selective sentencing policy. In this chapter, the implications of this study's findings for current models used to estimate incapacitative effects will be reviewed, and some estimates of these effects based on actual arrests occurring after release from prison will be presented.[1]

Models used to estimate the effects of selective incapacitation assume the existence of a *stable core of high-rate offenders* who would be the targets of such a policy. The average offense rates for these offenders are used to estimate the number of crimes that would be avoided by setting their terms of incarceration (when and if they occur) to specified lengths.[2] Similar information concerning offenders with lower rates of offending could be used to determine the relative payoff of increased incarceration for the high-rate offenders. Given this estimated benefit of the policy, decisions could be made as to whether the payoff would be great enough to warrant trying to identify those (relatively rare) high-rate offenders and keep them locked up.

Without the assumption of offense-rate stability, these models have little meaning. They might still be able to provide information on what would happen if high-rate offenders were incarcerated during the periods of time when they were, indeed, committing crimes at relatively high rates, but it would have to be understood that at each point in time, different offenders would be involved. In addition, the policy implied in such estimates would involve identifying the offenders who would have the highest rates during that period of time when they might be incapacitated: immediately following a major conviction (and its accompanying sentence, if any). Studies, including the present one, which have attempted to predict offense rates or arrest rates during this postrelease period have not, to date, met with a great deal of success.

The present data have shown that, for the serious offenders included in the sample, arrest rates (and presumably offense rates) were not very stable or predictable. Offenders did not maintain particular arrest rates throughout their careers. There were also few clues in their records that would enable an accurate prediction of what their rates of arrest would be during particular periods. This instability and unpredictability was most marked precisely at the point at which a selective incapacitation policy would be applied: after a given sentence was served.

Thus, estimates of the effects of a policy of selective incapacitation for these offenders using the aforementioned models would not be expected to be very meaningful. However, rough estimates of what the possible effects

---

[1] The analyses discussed in this chapter were performed for all cases with adult prison terms—former CYA cases and the supplementary sample obtained from the California Department of Corrections (CDC). This sample of cases with adult prison terms will be referred to at times as the CDC sample.

[2] Other assumptions, such as the assumption of constant probabilities of arrest (given the commission of a crime), conviction (given an arrest), and incarceration (once convicted), are also normally used with these models. These assumptions, however, are not crucial, since it is theoretically possible to incorporate conditional probabilities (e.g., higher probabilities of prison terms for those with prior convictions) into the model. The validity of these assumptions could not be addressed with the present data.

of certain policies might have been for particular offenders can be made using the kinds of data available in this study: the number of arrests and the number of months each offender spent outside of incarceration during the period after release from prison. These figures were used to estimate the number of known crimes that might have been avoided for each year of additional incarceration time, if these offenders had been locked up for an additional year.

Since many of these offenders served some additional time during the first year after release, increasing their sentences by one more year would not, in general, have resulted in an extra year of incarceration. The average number of arrests occurring during that first 12 months after release would therefore have been an underestimate of the number of expected arrests averted per year of additional incarceration. First, the amount of added incarceration time resulting from a one-year increase in sentence length was calculated by substracting the number of months spent incarcerated during that year from 12. This figure was summed across offenders and divided by 12 to obtain the total number of additional *person-years* of incarceration that would have resulted from the one-year term increase for these offenders. The number of arrests divided by this figure provided an estimate of the number of known crimes that would have been prevented for each additional person-year of incarceration imposed on these offenders. This estimate is, of course, exactly equivalent to an aggregate street-time rate of arrest for that one-year period following release from prison.[3] Also of interest in these analyses were the percentages of the various groups that had *no arrests* during the period of hypothetical incapacitation; for these cases, no known crime-reduction benefit would have been obtained through their increased incarceration.

In estimating these potential incapacitation effects, it was assumed that additional time spent in prison would have had no effect on their behavior (arrest rate or length of criminal carreer) other than to prevent them from committing crimes for some specified length of time. Under this assumption, those crimes for which they were arrested during the hypothesized period of incapacitation would have been prevented, and the offenders would have proceeded with their criminal careers from that point on, as if that period had never been there. Of course, no basis exists for making such an assumption since there was no way of knowing what effect, if any, an

---

[3] The number of *crimes* potentially prevented through incapacitation would, in general, be larger than the number of arrests, since not all crimes result in arrests. The appropriate multiplier to use in translating arrests into crimes, however, is not known. Estimates based on the probability of arrest vary considerably across jurisdictions and among crimes (Blumstein et al., 1986) and may be different for the period of parole supervision following prison. No attempt will be made, therefore, to extrapolate from arrests to crimes in this discussion of findings. The reader should bear in mind, however, that the incapacitation effects, in terms of the estimated number of *crimes* prevented, would be larger than the present estimates based on *arrests*.

additional year of prison would have had on these offenders, but any other assumption would be equally unsupported by empirical evidence. The issue is an important one, however, and deserves considerable attention if one is to fully understand the potential effects of selective sentencing policies. It was also assumed that the incapacitated offenders would not have been replaced by others and that their crimes were not committed as members of groups that would have committed those crimes even without the offender who was incapacitated. To date, little is known about the extent to which these assumptions hold (Cohen, 1983).[4] Consequently, the present (and all other) estimates of the effects of incapacitation on overall levels of crime must be interpreted very cautiously.

The above calculations were performed both for total offenses and violent offenses. These estimates were derived not only for the total sample but for various subsamples as well, in order to explore the relative effectiveness of alternative policies of selective incapacitation.These estimated incapacitation effects provide an overview of what might be expected from policies aimed at incapacitating various types of offenders. These estimates may also provide a basis for understanding what might be the effect of letting certain kinds of offenders out of prison early: the number of extra crimes expected for each person-year of prison time not served.

To illustrate how data such as these might be used to understand the effects of particular policies of selective sentencing, the effects of letting some offenders out early while keeping other offenders in prison longer were then estimated. For example, under one hypothetical policy, offenders with high rates of arrest in the Pre period would serve an additional year, while those with low rates of arrest served one year less. Assuming that an equal number were released early as kept longer, the overall effect on prison space, jail time, and arrests could be estimated. These analyses provide a rough indication of what might be expected from such a policy if it were exercised without regard to other factors, such as seriousness of crime, nature of prison behavior, and so on.

Incapacitation Effects for Various Offenders

As an aid in understanding the potential effects of incapacitating particular types of offenders identifiable prior to their release from prison, estimates were first made of the effects of incapacitating *all* offenders (collective

---

[4] Replacement or ongoing group crime might seem more likely with respect to property crimes, which are driven more by market considerations (the demand for drugs, for example, or organized recruitment by "fences"). Violent crimes, which tend to occur between acquaintances, may be more vulnerable to incapacitating particular offenders, but a good portion of these crimes seem to be related to other, more economic, criminal activities (bad drug deals) as well.

incapacitation) and of incapacitating those offenders with the highest rates of arrest during the post-release period. Presumably, the purpose of *selective* incapacitation is to improve on what would be obtained from simply keeping all offenders in prison for an extra year. The estimated effects of collective incapacitation policies can therefore be considered as a kind of minimal effect against which to evaluate the effects of incapacitating particular types of offenders. Further, the best one could expect from such a policy would be that it perfectly selected those offenders with the highest rates of postrelease criminal behavior. The estimated incapacitation effects for these offenders can serve as an estimate of the "upper limit" of what any policy might achieve with offenders of the kind in this sample.

Table 9.1 shows the incapacitation effect estimates for all cases in the sample, based on increasing all sentences by one to four years. Also shown in this table are the estimated effects of incapacitating (for one additional year) those offenders with low, medium, or high rates of total or violent arrests during the four-year Post period. For the 607 cases with at least 12 months of follow-up after release, 1230 arrests were recorded during that 12 months (an average of 2.03 per offender). Since some of these offenders went

TABLE 9.1 Incapacitation effects of increased CDC terms: No selection versus perfect prediction.

		Total offenses			Violent offenses		
	N of cases	Arrests	Per added year	% no arrests	Arrests	Per added year	% no arrests
Additional Years							
One	607[a]	1230	2.52	30.1%	264	.54	72.7%
Two	579	2083	2.51	18.7%	427	.52	59.8%
Three	550	2755	2.50	12.5%	529	.48	52.2%
Four	512	3158	2.39	9.2%	621	.47	46.9%
Differences by Post Arrest Rate (one added year)							
Total offenses							
Low	176[b]	87	.53	69.3%	24	.15	89.8%
Medium	215	383	2.15	19.1%	93	.52	69.1%
High	194	695	4.94	9.8%	112	.80	66.5%
Violent offenses							
Low	280	411	1.75	45.0%	0	—	100.0%
Medium	111	180	1.84	25.2%	47	.48	62.2%
High	194	574	3.83	14.4%	182	1.21	44.8%

[a] Only those cases with full years of follow-up were included in these estimates.
[b] Cases with less than 12 months of street time during the four-year post-release period did not have arrest rates calculated and were not included here.

to jail or back to prison during that first year, the sample accumulated less than one person-year of street time per offender. Consequently, a higher number of arrests (2.52) occurred for each person-year of street time during that first year out of prison. Thus, if all of those offenders had been released one year later, 2.52 arrests would have been prevented for each additional person-year of incarceration imposed on the sample. Of the arrests occurring during that period, 264 were for violent offenses (.43 per offender, on average). If an additional year had been added to the sentences of these offenders, these violent crimes would have been prevented at the rate of around one for every two person-years of additional incarceration. Finally, about 30% of these offenders would have been incarcerated even though they would have committed no known crimes during that 12 months.

In Chapter 7, aggregate arrest rates were found to remain fairly steady during the four years following release from prison. It comes as no surprise, therefore, that the estimated effects of collective incapacitation remained more-or-less unchanged through up to four year of added prison time. If those 512 offenders who had four years of follow-up time had been kept in prison for four more years, about 2.4 arrests would have been prevented for every additional person-year they spent incarcerated, compared to 2.5 for the first year only. Over that four years, 3158 arrests would have been prevented, 621 of which would have been for violent offenses, and only 9.2% of these offenders would have been incarcerated despite the fact they would not have beeen arrested during that period.

The prevention of over two arrests per offender through adding a year to their prison sentences would seem like a sizable effect, especially considering that the number of crimes would be larger than the number of arrests and the number of offenders released from prison every year is substantial. For example, if this sample of prisoners was assumed to be representative of all adult prisoners in California in 1984, and prisoners were released from their initial sentences at the rate of about 20,000 per year,[5] over 40,500 known crimes would have been prevented by retaining those prisoners an extra year. Of those 40,500 crimes, about one-fifth (or 8700) would be for violent offenses. Preventing this number of crimes would have a substantial benefit for society, especially for the 8700 potential victims of violent crimes.

When this impact is viewed in the context of the total volume of crime in California, however, the effect appears much more modest. According to the 1984 Criminal Justice Profile, prepared by the California Department of Justice, there were slightly over 1,500,000 arrests reported by police department in 1984, around 113,000 of which were for violent offenses (as they are defined here). A reduction of 40,500 in this number would amount to a mere

---

[5] This figure was provided by the California Department of Corrections as an estimate of the number of individuals released to parole from their sentences (rather than from a parole revocation) during the 1984–85 fiscal year. It is 75% of the 26,000 offenders of all types released to parole in 1984–85.

2.7% decrease in the number of arrests and, presumably, in the number of crimes as well. Decreasing the number of violent crimes by 8700 would reduce the total volume of violent crime by only 7.7%. Thus, even a global policy of incapacitation aimed at adult prisoners would have only a small impact on the amount of crime in California.

An additional mitigating factor involves the cost associated with retaining those offenders the extra year. The average length of stay for the 607 offenders in the CDC sample was 34 months. During the first year out, each offender served, on average, 1.52 months of additional prison time (due to revocations of parole or new offenses), so that if sentences were increased by one year, an additional 10.48 months of prison time would have been served, on average, per offender. This added time would amount to a 31% increase in the prison terms of these offenders. For the 607 offenders in the sample, a total of 530 additional person-years would have been served in prison; at $15,000 per person-year (CDC estimate), the cost per arrest prevented would have been $15,000 × 530/1230, or $6463. The cost per violent arrest prevented would have been $30,114. Applying these figures to the release cohort of 20,000 offenders, the aforementioned 2.7% decrease in arrests would have occurred at a total cost of around 17,500 additional person-years of prison time, with a dollar cost of approximately $262,500,000.[6]

If all offenders in CDC institutions were like those in this sample and served similar amounts of time in prison (34 months on average), the 2.7% decrease in crime woud come at a cost of increasing the prison population by around 31%—the amount that each offender's term was increased. In fact, the current prison population is *not* like those studied here, and the dissimilarities would decrease any expected collective incapacitation benefits. Recent changes in California law have forced the imposition of prison sentences on greater proportions of offenders; as a consequence, the prison population has come increasingly to be made up of less serious offenders with shorter prison sentences. The current average length of stay, for example, is around 24 months, as compared to the 34 months served, on average, by the offenders in this sample (who mostly served their terms in the middle to late 1970s). For such a population, a somewhat lower number of arrests could be expected for each additional person-year of incarceration. More important, the size of the prison population could be expected to increase dramatically as a function of the increased length of stay. The addition of 12 months to an average term of 24 months would amount to a 50% increase in time served for each offender and a 50% increase in the prison population.

---

[6] These dollar figurs do not take into account cost savings associated with decreased jail time that would have been served during the period of incapacitation (approximately .8 months per offender in this sample) nor the savings associated with the offenders not serving those portions of later revocations or new prison commitments served in years beyond the first one after release. Such adjustments would have little impact on the overall cost ratio per arrest prevented.

Returning to Table 9.1, the estimated incapacitation effects for the offenders with the highest four-year Post arrest rates can be seen to be almost 10 times as high as the estimated effects for those with the lowest rates. Their incapacitation would prevent almost five arrests for every additional person-year of incarceration imposed—nearly double the rate for collective incapacitation— and only 9.8% of these offenders had no arrests during their first 12 months on the street. Although a slightly smaller proportion of these high-rate offenders' arrests were for violent crimes (16%, as opposed to 21% for the total sample), the number of violent arrests per person-year of additional incarceration would have been half again as high as for the total sample. A similar increase in efficiency would be obtained by selectively incapacitating only those offenders with the highest post-release rates of violent arrests.[7] The incapacitation effect for violent crimes would have more than doubled over that estimated for collective incapacitation, while the effect for total offenses would have been, again, around 1.5 times that obtained for all cases.

As promising as these figures appear, they should again he placed into the larger perspective. To achieve a 10% reduction in arrests in 1984, the number of arrests would have to have decreased by 150,000. At five arrests per person-year of additional incarceration, 30,000 person-year of incarceration would be required to produce that reduction. Since the offenders in the high-rate group served an average of nearly three months in prison or jail during the 12 months after release, an additional year of prison would produce an average of only .75 person-years of added incarceration per offender. At this rate, it would have taken 40,000 of these offenders, each retained in prison an extra year, to produce a 10% reduction in the number of arrests in California in 1984. Assuming that the distribution of arrest rates in the 1984 release cohort was similar to that in the present sample, the one-third with the highest rates would comprise only about 6700 offenders: one-sixth the number needed to generate the 10% reduction. In fact, incapacitating these 6700 high-rate offenders for another year would be expected to prevent approximately $695/194 = 3.58$ arrests per offender, or around 24,000 arrests overall. That number is 1.6% of the total number of arrests in California in 1984. While crude, these estimates suggest that even with an incapacitation strategy perfectly targeted at the third with the highest post-release rates in 1984, less than a 2% reduction in overall crime would have been achieved.

It would appear that incapacitation strategies (whether collective or selective) aimed at offenders sentenced to adult prison could not be expected to substantially reduce crime in California. A more modest goal might be simply to increase the efficiency of whatever incapacitative effect is associated

---

[7] The intention was to divide the sample roughly into thirds, based on their rates of arrest, but since almost half (47.9%) had *no* violent arrests during the four-year period after release from CDC, such a division was not possible. It was decided, instead, to identify the top one-third as high-rate, leaving those with lower (but not zero) rates in the middle group. Low-rate, in the present context, means no violent arrests.

with prison use. As shown above, a perfect prediction device could identify a "high-rate" group of offenders for which incapacitation effects would have been 10 times as high as for the low-rate group. Sentencing based on such discriminations could greatly improve the overall crime-reduction payoff per person-year of prison time. Unfortunately, behavioral instability and the limits of predictability for these offenders suggest that such a perfect prediction device is not likely to appear in the near future. However, the potential payoffs of such strategies can be explored.

Shown in Table 9.2 are the estimated incapacitative effects associated with offenders with various characteristics: prior arrest rate, commitment offense,

TABLE 9.2 Incapacitation effects by various selection factors (term increased by one year).

		Total offenses			Violent offenses		
Selection factor	N of cases	Arrests	Per added year	% No arrests	Arrests	Per added year	% No arrests
Prior Offense Rate							
Total offenses							
Low	182	306	2.03	37.9%	60	.40	75.8%
Medium	197	387	2.37	29.4%	83	.51	74.1%
High	192	473	3.26	22.9%	106	.73	67.7%
Violent offenses							
Low	181	403	2.82	27.1%	46	.32	81.8%
Medium	206	393	2.33	30.6%	91	.54	73.3%
High	184	370	2.50	32.1%	112	.76	62.5%
Risk Score (Pre)							
Low	184	314	2.05	37.0%	76	.50	73.9%
Medium	178	364	2.46	29.2%	88	.59	68.5%
High	207	484	3.08	24.2%	85	.54	74.4%
Commitment Offense							
Homicide	31	44	1.65	51.6%	12	.45	74.2%
Rape	20	30	1.76	30.0%	12	.71	60.0%
Robbery	175	284	1.89	36.0%	97	.64	65.7%
Assault, other	64	141	2.62	25.0%	35	.65	71.9%
Burglary	161	336	2.81	28.0%	53	.44	77.6%
Other property	54	140	3.26	16.7%	23	.53	75.9%
Other	102	255	3.16	27.5%	32	.40	77.5%
Property Commitments Only							
Prior Rate (Total)							
Low	81	144	2.17	34.6%	26	.39	77.8%
Medium	115	254	2.82	24.3%	38	.42	78.3%
High	108	306	4.01	21.3%	42	.55	74.1%

[a] Only those cases with valid prior-rate levels were included.
[b] Cases missing any of the predictor variables were excluded.

and prediction score (from Chapter 8). These estimated effects can be compared to the "low" estimate, based on collective incapacitation, of 2.52 arrests per additional person-year of incarceration and the "high" estimate, based on perfect prediction, of 4.94 arrests per person-year. For all the CDC cases together, none of the estimated incapacitative effects is above the 3.73 midpoint between these two estimates, although some discrimination is indicated, particularly for prior arrest rate (total offenses). This variable served as a better discriminator than did the simple scale focusing on Prior factors that was derived from regression results.[8] For those offenders with the highest rates of arrest prior to entering prison, 3.26 arrests per person-year of additional incarceration would have been prevented by increasing their terms by one year, as compared to 2.03 for the low prior-rate offenders. A similar increase in efficiency would be obtained with this strategy with respect to preventing violent crimes as well. Distinctions based on the rate of prior violent arrests showed only a slight increase in potential efficiency with respect to violent offenses over that provided by total prior arrest rates, and showed no potential benefit with respect to total arrests.

Estimated incapacitative effects for total arrests showed an inverse relationship to seriousness of commitment offense. Those committed for homicide were arrested, on average, 1.65 times for every year of street time they accumulated, while "other property" offenders (grand theft, forgery, receiving stolen property, etc.) were arrested at nearly twice that rate (3.26 arrests per person-year). Such a relationship poses certain problems for potential selective incapacitation policies, since it implies that to maximize the crime-reduction benefits of prison, less serious property offenders should remain in prison longer than murderers, rapists, and robbers. At the least, it would suggest that selective sentencing policies based on risk may have to exclude these more serious cases from consideration; for example, a policy might be designed to set differential sentences for property offenders only. While a smaller amount of total crime could be reduced by such a restricted policy, it would be easier to implement, since it would not conflict so clearly with ordinary notions of "just deserts."

Also included in Table 9.2, for purposes of discussion, are the estimated incapacitative effects for those not committed for a violent offense (shown on the table as "Property Commitments Only"). These offenders were grouped according to their prior arrest rates, using the same cut-off points as for the entire sample. Notice first that there were relatively fewer low-rate arrestees in this subsample than in the larger sample; prior record was apparently more important for determining prison sentences for property offenders than for violent offenders. Second, the estimated incapacitative effects were higher for each prior-rate level than for the larger sample, indicating that violent

---

[8] Evidently, whatever power that was gained by including information on prior drug use was lost by reducing the distinctions based on prior arrest rate simply to "high-rate" vs. "others."

offenders at all levels of prior arrest rate were somewhat better risks during the first year after release. The estimated number of crimes that would have been prevented per person-year of additional incarceration for the high-rate offenders was 4.06, compared to 3.26 for the whole sample. The average number of arrests per offender during that period was somewhat lower: 2.83, as compared to 2.46 for the larger sample. Third, the difference between the estimated effects (total offenses) for high-rate and low-rate offenders was greater than for the total sample: 1.84 arrests per person-year difference versus 1.22 arrests. Finally, while differences were greater for total arrests, differences between high-rate and low-rate offenders in terms of estimated incapacitative effects relative to violent arrests were considerably smaller. Thus, by excluding offenders committed for violent offenses, greater incapacitative effect estimates were found for total offenses, but smaller effects were estimated for subsequent violent offenses.

Offenders committed for nonviolent offenses comprised a little over half (52%) of this sample of adult prisoners. The top third of these cases, then, would constitute about one-sixth of the sample. If the offenders paroled from CDC in 1984 had been similar to the present sample of CDC cases and have been incapacitated based on their prior records, approximately 3300 nonviolent, high-rate offenders would have been involved. At the rate of 2.83 offenses per offender, such a policy would have prevented only about 9350 Total arrests—0.6% of all arrests in California during that year. Even though the incapacitative payoff *per offender* appears fairly high for these cases, there simply would not be enough of them released from prison to make a big difference in the overall amount of crime in California.

Effects of Incapacitation on Crime and Incarceration

One way to evaluate incapacitation strategies is to assess their probable effects on the amount of crime and incarceration time associated with all CDC offenders in the sample over the length of the follow-up period. During that period, the 607 offenders in this sample who served adult prison terms (and who had at least 12 months of follow-up after release from prison) accumulated:

14,063   Total arrests
 2,628   Violent arrests
   545.2 Person-years of jail time
 1,759.3 Person-years of prison time
 2,304.6 Person-years of incarceration time

The estimated number of crimes and of person-years of jail, prison, and incarceration time associated with incapacitating various subgroups were divided by these figures, to get an estimate of the percentage of change associated with an incapacitative strategy that was focused on those offenders.

These percentages, of course, would refer to the effect of applying the strategy only once for each offender—at the time of the first prison term—and must be considered only rough estimates of the net effects of applying such a strategy to all prison terms.[9] For example, if the entire sample had been left in prison one more year, 1230 total and 264 violent arrests would have been prevented (from Table 9.1); these numbers constitute 8.7% of all crimes and 10.0% of all violent crimes, respectively. While this sample would have spent an additional 607 person-years in prison, they would *not* have spent some 40.8 person-years of jail time and 77.2 person-years of prison time (time that was served by these cases during that 12-month period). Thus, there would have been a net decrease of 40.8 person-years (or 7.5%) in the amount of jail time spent by these offenders, a net increase of $607 - 77.2 = 529.8$ person-years of prison time (an increase of 30.1%), and a net increase in overall incarceration time of $607 - 118.0 = 489$ person-years (21.2%).

These percentages, along with percentages for various subgroups, are shown in Table 9.3. All the figures assume a 12-month increase in prison terms and no other effects of the added prison time. Note that they are not weighted for sample size, so that differences among groups reflect, to some extent, differences in the size of the subgroup; for example, the "Medium" group for Post-period arrest rate for violent offenses was only about 40% as large as the "Low" group, so that even though the incapacitation effect per person-year is greater for these cases, a smaller percentage of crimes would be prevented by their incapacitation. These percentages merely provide a rough basis of comparison across subgroups; their usefulness is primarily in understanding the trade-offs for each separate subgroup. However, since the three high-arrest-rate groups have about the same number of cases, some comparisons can be made among them.

Among the groups identified on the basis of their Post-period rates of arrest for all offenses, retaining the 194 high-rate offenders in prison an extra year would have reduced the number of arrests for the entire CDC sample by almost 5%, while the amount of time spent in prison by this sample would have increased by 9%. Taking into account the savings in jail time, the increase in overall incarceration time for these offenders would have been about 6%. Since selective incapacitation would optimally target these high-rate offenders, these figures represent the maximum benefit that could have been obtained with this sample. In contrast, the incapacitation of the slightly larger number of medium-rate offenders would have decreased total arrests by only 2.7% while increasing prison time by almost 11%.

Incapacitating an equal sized group of the highest-rate violent offenders

---

[9] Applying the one-year increase to each term would tend to increase each of the percentages. However, due to the decrease in rates of arrest by age, a smaller incapacitative effect for later prison terms would be expected. Thus, the inclusion of later terms would be expected to result in smaller increases in the percentage of crimes prevented than in the amount of extra incarceration time.

TABLE 9.3 Effects of increased prison terms on crimes and incarceration: Various selection factors.

	N of Cases	Reductions			Increases	
		Total arrests	Violent arrests	Jail time	Prison time	Incarc. time
All Prison Cases[a]	607	8.8%	10.0%	7.5%	30.1%	21.2%
Post-rate Level						
Total offenses[b]						
Low	176	.6%	.9%	.6%	9.5%	7.1%
Medium	215	2.7%	3.5%	2.3%	10.8%	7.7%
High	194	4.9%	4.3%	3.3%	9.0%	6.1%
Violent offenses[b]						
Low	280	2.9%	—	2.1%	14.0%	10.2%
Medium	111	1.3%	1.8%	1.3%	6.0%	4.3%
High	194	4.1%	6.9%	2.8%	9.4%	6.5%
Pre-rate Level (Total Offenses)						
All cases[c]						
Low	182	2.2%	2.3%	1.8%	9.1%	6.6%
Medium	197	2.8%	3.2%	2.1%	9.9%	7.1%
High	192	3.4%	4.0%	3.2%	9.2%	6.3%
Property comm. only						
Low	81	1.0%	1.0%	.9%	4.0%	2.9%
Medium	115	1.8%	1.4%	1.4%	5.5%	3.9%
High	108	2.2%	6.6%	2.1%	5.0%	3.3%

[a] Only those cases with full years of follow-up were included in these estimates.
[b] Cases with less than 12 months of street time during the four-year post release period did not have arrest rates calculated and were not included here.
[c] Cases with less than 12 months of street time during the four-year pre prison period did not have arrest rates calculated and were not included here.

would have had a considerably greater impact on violent arrests for this sample (6.9% reduction, as opposed to 4.3% for the high-rate total group). A slightly smaller benefit would have been obtained for these offenders relative to total arrests. Since the high-rate violent offenders spent a somewhat smaller portion of their first year after release back in jail or prison, a slightly larger net increase in prison and incarceration time would have resulted from keeping them in prison the extra year.

Judged against these figures for the Post period, high-rate groups, the percentages associated with the Pre period, high-rate group do not appear so different. The percentage reductions in jail time and the percentage increase in prison and total incarceration time were very similar for low-, and high-rate groups. Reading down the columns for the Pre-rate level groups, it is apparent that a greater trade-off, in terms of potential crime reduction for the same increase in prison use, could be realized simply by sentencing based on prior rates of behavior. Note, moreover, that although the actual estimated reductions are small, the estimated reduction in violent crimes for the Pre high-rate group is remarkably close to that for the Post high-rate group. For total offenses, the reduction for the Pre high-rate group is only 70% as high as for the Post high-rate group.

As would be expected, the figures for those committed for nonviolent offenses (roughly half the sample) showed a slight increase in efficiency for reducing overall levels of arrest for this sample and slightly lower efficiency relative to violent offenses. By so restricting the eligible sample, however, only 2.2% of all arrests for the sample would have been prevented by incapacitating the higest-rate offenders.

These findings suggests that an incapacitative strategy aimed at increasing the lengths of stay of offenders already sentenced to prison is not likely to have a major effect on overall levels of crime in society. While some increase in efficiency can be obtained by identifying certain kinds of offenders for increased sentences, no group is large enough to account for much of the total crime. Perhaps a better way to evaluate incapacitation strategies is simply in terms of their ability to maximize the efficiency of prison use. Differences in the crimes-per-added-year bear on this issue. Of more direct relevance, however, would be estimates of the trade-offs that might be associated with strategies that increase sentences for some offenders and reduce them for others, with the overall aim of increasing public protection without increasing prison populations.

As mentioned earlier, data on crimes and incarceration occuring during the first 12 months after release might be used as a rough estimate not only of possible incapacitation effects, but also of what might be the result of releasing particular offenders one year earlier. In other words, if the 182 offenders with low rates of arrest during the Prior period were released 12 months early, an estimated additional 306 arrests (from Table 9.2) would occur. If, at the same time, the high-rate offenders were retained a year longer, an estimated 473 arrests would have been prevented, for a net reduction of 167 arrests. Since some were released and others retained, only a slight effect on prison populations would be expected.

An even clearer picture of the potential trade-offs would be obtained if these figures are standardized, so that they reflected the estimated number of crimes and person-years of incarceration added or prevented per 1000 offenders. This kind of analysis was performed for two hypothetical sentencing strategies: one based on releasing 1000 offenders 12 months early and retaining 1000 offenders 12 months longer, and one based on maintaining prison populations as close to present levels as possible. The results are shown in Table 9.4.

In both cases, offenders with low rates of arrest in the Prior period were released 12 months early, while high-rate offenders were retained an additional 12 months. In one case, all offenders were considered eligible; the other was restricted to offenders sentenced for nonviolent crimes. It was assumed that those released early would commit crimes and spend time in jail or prison as they actually did during their first 12 months out of prison (adding those

TABLE 9.4 Net effects of increasing terms for high-rate offenders and decreasing terms for low-rate offenders (sentence changed by 12 months).

	Total arrests	Violent arrests	Jail years	Prison years used $(+)$ or saved $(-)$
All Commitments				
1000 in each group				
Low-rate	$+1681$	$+330$	$+53.3$	$+117.0 - 1000 = -883.0$
High-rate	-2463	-552	-90.1	$-153.6 + 1000 = +846.4$
Net change	-782	-222	-36.8	-36.6
Steady-state Level				
Low-rate $(n = 958)$	$+1610$	$+316$	$+51.1$	$+112.1 - 958 = -845.9$
High-rate $(n = 1000)$	-2463	-552	-90.1	$-153.6 + 1000 = +846.4$
Net change	-853	-236	-39.0	$+0.5$
Property Commitments Only				
1000 in each group				
Low-rate	$+1778$	$+321$	$+58.6$	$+123.5 - 1000 = -876.5$
High-rate	-2833	-389	-105.6	$-188.9 + 1000 = +811.1$
Net change	-1055	-68	-47.0	-65.4
Steady-state level				
Low-rate $(n = 925)$	$+1644$	$+297$	$+54.2$	$+114.2 - 925 = -810.8$
High-rate $(n = 1000)$	-2833	-389	-105.6	$-188.9 + 1000 = +811.1$
Net change	-1189	-92	-51.4	$+0.3$

crimes and incarcerations to their totals). It was also assumed that incapacitating the other offenders would reduce the total volume of crime and incarceration time by the amounts actually accumulated during the first year after their release.

Standardization simply involved dividing 1000 by the number of cases in each group and using the result as a multiplier for the other figures. For example, there were 182 cases with low rates of prior arrests, and they were arrested 306 times during the one-year period following release. If 1000 of such cases had been released, they would have been arrested an estimated $1000/182 \times 306 = 1681$ times. Similar calculations were used to estimate the number of violent arrests and person-years of jail time (each of which would be increased by letting some offenders out early and decreased by holding other offenders longer).

The calculation of prison time involved, first, estimating the amount of time each group would have spent back in prison (as above), and then subtracting that amount from the number of offenders involved (since each would contribute one person-year of additional, or "saved," prison time). Using the earlier example, the 182 low-rate offenders accumulated 21.3 years of prison time their first year out; based on a sample of 1000, that number would have been 117.0 person-years. By releasing these cases early, 1000 person-years would have been saved, but since they could be expected to serve 117 person-years even though they were released early, the net savings would be $1000 - 117 = 883$ person-years. On the other side, those high-rate offenders retained longer would have used 1000 additional person-years of prison, but would *not* have served 153.7 person-years, for a net increase of 846.3 person-years of prison.

Using these estimates, the net effect of letting 1000 low-rate cases out early and retaining 1000 high-rate cases longer was calculated; for all cases, an estimated 782 fewer arrests would have occurred (222 violent arrests), 36.8 fewer person-years of jail time would have been served, and 36.6 fewer person-years of prison time would have been served. Similar estimates for property offenders only showed that considerably more total arrests, but fewer violent arrests, would have been prevented. In addition, a greater net savings in prison use would have been realized.

The "steady-state" calculations involved determining a multiplier that would produce an overall prison savings estimate that was similar to the prison-use estimate found for the 1000 high-rate offenders in each analysis. Simple algebraic calculations identified the proper number of "releasees" for all cases to be 958, and for property offenders only, 925. Thus, if 958 low-rate cases were released early for every 1000 high-rate offenders retained, estimated prison use and savings would nearly cancel out. Since fewer cases were released, the total net reduction in crimes and jail-time would have been higher: such a sentencing strategy could have prevented around 850 arrests and 39 person-years of jail time for every 1000 high-rate cases incapacitated, with no increase in prison use.

The number of arrests prevented by such a strategy would still be minuscule, of course, as a fraction of all arrests in California; even if 10,000 of these offenders per year were incapacitated under such a policy, less than 9000 arrests per year would be prevented (0.6% of the arrests in California during 1984). Nevertheless, a reduction in the number of crimes at minimal cost to society may be considered worthwhile simply on the basis of the greater efficiency in the use of scarce prison resources.

Summary

These findings suggest that while incapacitative effects differ for various kinds of offenders, little in the way of real impact on overall levels of crime could be achieved through incapacitation alone. Even collective incapacitation (holding *every offender* for an additional year) would probably not have produced a 3% reduction in California arrests in 1984. Bearing in mind the rather tenuous assumptions on which even these simple estimates were based (no replacement and no groups continuing to commit crimes in the absence of particular members), they are more likely to be overestimates of incapacitative effects than underestimates. Considering, in addition, that current prison populations are probably made up of less serious offenders than those included in these analyses, the hopes of significantly reducing crime through incapacitation, whether collective or selective, would appear remote. Clearly, however, the data support the notion (under the very stringent assumption that no one else would have committed these crimes) that some increase in efficiency might possibly be obtained by enhancing or reducing sentences based on prior rate of arrest (or convictions or some other predictive device). For offenders like those in this sample, over two arrests could possibly have been prevented for every additional person-year of incarceration. Whether other offenders would be arrested in their places is uncertain.

Incapacitation is not the only effect that prison may have on offenders, of course, and these analyses did not directly address any other possible effects. However, one major reason that incapacitation effects were not very high for these offenders is that arrest rates were relatively low during the period following the prison term, as noted in Chapter 7. Incarceration seemed to have a "suppression effect" on the criminal behavior of these offenders, perhaps through deterrence or rehabilitation, reducing the potential incapacitative effects. Whether, and how much, any *changes* in the length of prison terms might alter this suppression effect is not known.

Chapter 10
Summary and Discussion

This study was undertaken to assess the resonableness of certain major assumptions underlying the concept of selective incapacitation and recent research on that topic, particularly the research that relies on statistical models of crime and the criminal justice system. The main assumption, in this regard, was that criminal careers are characterized by a reasonably constant rate of criminal behavior.[1] High-volume offenders, who are the primary targets of hypothetical selective sentencing policies, are assumed to contribute their disproportionate share of crimes by maintaining a relatively high rate of criminal activity throughout their active adult criminal careers. Other offenders, in the meantime, plod along at lower, but constant, rates of criminal behavior throughout their careers as well. This primary assumption has several important corollaries: that offense rates do not decline with age; that interventions, such as probation, prison, or any form of treatment, will not affect offense rates appreciably; and that these rates will not change as a result of *other* offenders being treated in one way or another by the criminal justice system. Under these assumptions, selective incapacitation appears not only to have potential for reducing crime, but appears to be the *only* way of coping with the crime problem.

Coincidentally, this same assumption, with its corollaries, underlies the use of statistical models of the crime/response process. Under this assumption, offense rates can be expected to remain constant regardless of how one tinkers with the criminal justice system, and incapacitation effects can be estimated as a direct function of the amount of time offenders (with various rates) remain behind bars. While few criminologists take these assumptions, as such, too seriously, some do take these *models* seriously, estimating (or re-estimating) incapacitation effects based on selective sentencing policies (Greenwood, 1982; Cohen 1983, 1986; Visher, 1986). In so doing, they implicitly accept the assumptions of the method, for without these assumptions, the estimates

---

[1] This study could not address the more critical assumption that the crimes that would have been commited by incarcerated offenders would not simply be committed by others instead.

derived from the models have little meaning. If offense rates change, incapacitation effects would depend on the factors associated with that change (such as the age of the offender). If these rates are simply unstable, or related to a large number of factors, the effects of lengthening terms for particular offenders would be impossible to estimate with enough precision to make the models very useful.

Now, if offense rates are stable for individual offenders, offense rates would not be expected to vary by age for offenders who were active in crime. Nor would it be expected that rates would differ by race, although the reasons are not so obvious. To assume that rates are stable is, in effect, to deny that social circumstances affect the level of criminal activity, other than to cause minor variations in an otherwise constant pattern of activity. Conversely, to accept that rates of criminal behavior are socially determined is to accept the likelihood that they would change over time (i.e., be unstable). Differences by race would suggest either that social circumstances *do* have an effect on rates of criminal behavior or that ethnic groups differ with respect to some "natural" inclination toward committing crimes. Neither of these possibilities is particularly pleasant for the proponents of selective incapacitation or the users of models that make the same assumption of stability.

In the present study, the issue of offense rate stability, both directly and with respect to the relationship of these rates to race and age, was the primary focus. Data were collected for a large sample of serious offenders, most of whom were institutionalized as wards of the California Youth Authority during the 1960s. Information on officially recorded crimes and any available information on background characteristics and on adult drug use, marital status and employment were coded for a 15 to 20 year adult period. Criminal behavior patterns were analyzed for the entire adult career, for the period up to the last recorded arrest (the "active" criminal period), for random "halves" of each offender's career (odd ages and even ages), for four-year blocks of time, and, for most cases, for the four-year periods immediately preceding and following a known adult incarceration. These analyses provided a rather detailed picture of how the known criminal behavior of this sample differed among offenders and over time. In addition, the usefulness of available information on noncriminal activities for identifying offenders with high rates of criminal behavior was assessed, and some direct estimates of the amount of crime that could have been prevented by lengthening the prison sentences served by these offenders were derived.

In Chapters 3 and 4, it was shown that, for this large sample of serious offenders, both the kinds of crimes for which they were arrested and the rate of arrest clearly differed by race and clearly declined with age. These data suggest that criminal behavior cannot simply be regarded as a manifestation of immutable individual differences, unaffected by social forces or situational factors. Social influences related to ethnicity or age appear to affect not only whether, when, and for how long offenders engage in criminal careers, but also the year-to-year nature and intensity of those careers. Considering that these influences may change as circumstances change for these individual offenders, it would be expected that offense rates would not only decline over time, but would also be unstable.

Some indication of how changeable these rates were for these offenders was found in the analysis of individual stability (Chapter 6). One analysis focused on the extent to which offenders with higher rates maintained higher rates than other offenders, even though average rates were declining over time (relative stability). Another analysis focused on the extent to which high-rate offenders, those in the top third, continued to have high rates of arrest (absolute stability). In both analyses, arrest rates were found to show considerable instability from one four-year block of time to the next. Although unreliability of official arrest rates, as a measure of actual criminal behavior, would tend to make offense rates appear less stable over time than they actually were, the amount of observed instability was greater than might be expected based simply on unreliability alone. Further, the longer these four-year periods were apart, the lower the stability; if measurement error alone was involved, the observed stability may have been low, but would not have decreased as the time between the two measurement periods increased.

Patterns over time showed that few offenders maintained a consistent pattern of being in the lowest, middle, or highest third of the sample in terms of their rates of arrest over four-year periods. The least stability in this regard was found for having a high rate. While most of the sample had at least one four-year period in which their rates of arrest were among the highest third, only a minority of these (28% over three periods and 12% over four periods) were in the highest third over *most* of these periods. These findings suggest that to the extent that this kind of instability is generalizable to other offenders, models that assume rates to be stable will overestimate the amount of crime that could be prevented by locking up individuals who, at particular times, were identified as high-rate offenders.

Further evidence of instability and its implications for selective sentencing policies came from the analysis of arrest rates before and after a sentence to probation or prison (Chapter 7). Consistent with earlier findings concerning total careers, differences in the rates of violent arrests were found among ethnic groups both before and after incarceration (if any), and arrest rates were found to generally decline with age. These trends once again point to social influences, and suggest that even for these most serious members of the sample, individual rates of criminal behavior depended on the offender's circumstances.

In addition, two important patterns were found. On the one hand, rates of arrest showed a clear *increase* during the four years immediately prior to incarceration, suggesting that these offenders were incarcerated and/or sentenced to probation typically after a relatively short-term acceleration in criminal behavior (including crimes serious enough to warrant such sanctions). This uncharacteristic increase in criminal activity strongly suggests the importance of short-term situational influences in determining rates of criminal behavior. It also suggests that this pre-incarceration period would be most inappropriate for establishing typical levels or distributions of offense rates.

On the other hand, arrest rates observed for the years following release from incarceration showed them to be generally lower than would be expected simply because these offenders got older. During the first year out, rates for former prison inmates were lower than at any point during the four years prior to prison; rates for those sentenced to jail or probation also showed a decline, although not as marked. In both cases, the rates continued to decline during the four years after release. The course these careers would have taken in the absence of these official responses cannot be determined, but it is possible that the incarceration pevented a continued acceleration in behavior, especially for those sentenced to prison. If so, the crime-reduction benefits of existing incarceration policies may not be fully understood or appreciated. In addition, the fact that these offenders displayed lowered activity levels following release from jail or prison suggests that extending prison sentences would have less of an effect on crime than might be expected from estimates of criminal activity based on preincarceration arrests.

As one might expect from these trends, the correspondence of rate levels (correlations of rates or agreement on trichotomized rate levels) from pre-incarceration to post-incarceration was very low: lower than for adjacent four-year blocks of time and much lower than would be expected based on unreliability alone. Correlations and simple tabulations showed that differences among offenders during the pre-incarceration period were not very indicative of what those differences were during the post-incarceration period. For example, of those offenders who had the highest rates of arrest prior to prison, only 40% were among the highest third after release, as compared to almost 30% of those who were *not* high-rate prior to prison. Thus, the official data on criminal behavior would have been the least useful in identifying future high-rate offenders in this sample precisely at that point when these data would most likely have been used.

In general, instability and the measurement problems associated with using official data greatly reduce the ability to identify which offenders would have had the highest offense rates during any particular period. Predictions based on a wider variety of predictive factors, moreover, appeared to offer little hope for improving on this situation, since official data on criminality were all that were available for use as criterion (dependent) variables. Predictions useful for sentencing decisions must be made from information available from official sources. At the present time, it would appear that these data are simply not good enough to permit adequate prediction accuracy.

Predictions based on split-half measures (Chapter 5), wherein the underlying criminal career was divided into two random "samples" of the offender's yearly arrests, should have been very good: limited only by the effects of measurement error and random fluctuations in criminal behavior. Instead, arrest rates in each half of the career accounted for only about one-half the variance in arrest rates for the other half; adding other predictors to the equation increased the explained variation only a few percent. These findings suggest that even if criminal behavior was stable, random "noise" caused by measurement error alone would be enough to make the identification of high-rate offenders problematic.

When instability was added, accurate prediction of arrest rates became difficult indeed using these data: predictions of criminal behavior during the period after release from prison was low. While many interesting bivariate (two-variable) relationships were found, predictions of post-release arrest rates accounted for only 16 to 18% of the variance in these rates for all cases together, and around 10% of the variance for those cases with adult prison terms. On cross-validation, the prediction accuracy dropped even further. Part of this inability to predict was, again, due the unreliability of arrest rates, but regardless of the reason, this low predictability precluded accurate identification of postrelease, high-rate offenders in this sample.

Finally, the study addressed the issue of whether selective incapacitation has the *potential* of reducing crime or serving as the basis of greater efficiency in the use of scarce prison resources. Using information on the amount of time each offender spent in custody during the 12-month period after rlease from prison and the number of arrests occurring during that period, estimates were made of the potential effects of incapacitating all offenders—or offenders of particular types—for an additional year (Chapter 9). The analysis showed that even the "best" (most efficient) policies would not have prevented a significant amount of crime. If *all* offenders were kept an additional year, only about a 3% reduction in crime could have been achieved. If the offenders with the highest postprison rates were incapacitated (if prediction were perfect), the reduction in crimes would have been less than 2%. Other analyses suggested that selective sentencing policies could have provided for some reduction in arrests with no increase in prison populations, but the overall reduction would have been less than 1000 arrests for every 3000 prisoners subjected to the policy. Consequently, while there was some indication that prison space could be more efficiently used, a significant impact of selective incapacitation on overall levels of crime in society appears unlikely.

Policy Implications

To the extent that these findings are generalizable to other offenders, they, along with the results of those analyses fucusing on potential incapacitative effects, suggest certain policy implications:

1. Selective incapacitation policies hold only minimal potential for reducing levels of crime in society. Analyses fucusing on incapacitation effects suggested that longer sentences for offenders going to prison would have only a small impact on overall crime in society. Selective sentencing policies

may increase the efficiency of prison use to some extent, but would not produce a substantial reduction in the number of crimes committed in the wider society.

2. The actual incapacitative effects of policies of selective sentencing will be difficult to estimate but will, in any case, be lower than might be expected based on the recent (pre-prison) criminal behavior of the "high-rate" offenders. The unreliability of official records, general declines with age, and instability in criminal behavior combine to lower the expected offense rates for offenders identified as "high-rate" on the basis of their arrest histories. These problems appear especially important at the time of a major conviction—the point at which sentencing decisions would be made. Models that assume offense rates to be stable would be of little help in estimating these effects, even if declines in these rates by age were incorporated into the model.

3. While factors related to "risk" of future high-rate criminal behavior can be identified, the accurate identification of high-rate offenders using information available in official records does not appear possible at present. Predictive analyses are hindered by the unreliability of arrest rates, as measures of underlying criminal propensity, as well as by instability in criminal behavior. These problems are not so serious that they prevent the identification of factors that increase the probability ("risk") of engaging in criminal behavior at high rates. However, predictive devices using these factors can be expected to produce a large proportion of false predictions. Such devices must be employed cautiously.

Research Implications

These findings also suggest certain implications for future research in criminology:

1. The period immediately prior to a major conviction may be the least useful for studying patterns of criminal behavior. Arrest rates during this period were found to be relatively uncharacteristic of overall patterns of criminal behavior for these offenders.

2. There appear to be upper limits to the prediction accuracy that can be obtained using official offense data. While these limits do not preclude the usefulness of official data for identifying factors that influence criminal behavior, the ability to account for even most of the differences in levels of criminal behavior among offenders using official data is probably an unrealistic goal.

3. There is a need for research on the situational and/or circumstantial determinants of offense rates among offenders and over time. An understanding of these factors could pave the way toward social action or interventions that could reduce crime through reducing the number of

"high-rate" periods for particular offenders or within populations of offenders.

4. There is a need for a better understanding of the global effects of incarceration on criminal behavior. Needed is research on the patterns of activity and association prior to conviction and on the effect of incarceration on those patterns. If, for example, incarceration reduces crime through disrupting various crime-supporting situational or social influences, it might be possible to specify an optimum length of incarceration (how long it takes to produce this effect and the point at which no additional effects could be expected).

Implications for Understanding Criminal Careers

So far, the present findings have been discussed primarily in terms of what they suggest is *not* true of criminal careers: that these findings are not consistent with a conception of these careers as predominantly stable and predictable. The criminality within this sample of serious offenders was found to differ by race, to decline with age, to display a considerable amount of instability over time, to increase sharply immediately before major sentences and then decrease markedly immediately afterwards, and to have few solid predictors or correlates that would help to differentiate its relative levels. These characteristics seem to suggest a picture of criminal careers quite different from the rather static conception currently popular. In these remaining pages, this picture will be described and some of its implications for understanding the kinds of careers found for these offenders will be discussed.[2]

This conception starts with the premise that, for the most part, criminal behavior patterns can be understood in the same terms that noncriminal patterns are understood; that is, it assumes that people who commit crimes are not necessarily that different from other people. For most crimes (excluding those based on addiction—drug use—or those springing from severe mental abnormalities) no "special motivation" is required for understanding why they might be committed; remuneration, thrill, revenge, exercise of power, and so on, usually serve quite adequately.

What appears to distinguish criminals such as those in this sample from noncriminals is not so much the "ends" that are sought, but the inclusion of criminal "means" among their possible approaches to attaining those ends. The viability of criminal approaches, however, does not imply the consistent choice of those approaches. While crime may be seen as the most expeditious

---

[2] This discussion will be drawing loosely on "control theory" principles (Hirschi, 1969). Although this theory is certainly not the only basis for understanding or explaining crime or the career patterns of particular offenders, it does provide a convenient framework for understanding both the instability of these criminal careers and the importance of situational factors. As such, it can help to understand the "career" patterns of the offenders studied here.

and/or direct approach in a given instance ("to make a fast buck" expresses the common understanding of this kind of pragmatism, as does "to take matters into your own hands"), there is little about ordinary "street" criminality to recommend it as a *stable* part of a person's lifestyle. By and large, criminal behavior amounts to rather low-paying, high-risk, and typically unpleasant behavior. From a perspective that sees criminality as the inclusion of criminal behavior as one option for attaining desired ends, and, at the same time, views criminal behavior as a situationally expedient but generally unattractive option, the kinds of patterns of criminality found in the present study seem somewhat reasonable.

Hirschi, in presenting his "control theory" (Hirschi, 1969), suggests that motivation *to* commit crimes may not be as important for understanding or predicting crime as the *lack* of motivation *not to* commit crimes. This motivation to be law-abiding, further, springs from being imbedded in a complex network of social institutions and relationships. Involvement in *each of these* carries with it the expectation that the individual will generally adhere to the norms and laws of the society as well as to the norms and expectations associated with every other social institution in the network. The less deeply one is entrenched in the social network, the fewer the sources of expectations to conform, and the less one would have to lose by "cheating" at the social game—even by committing the unsavory and particularly unpleasant kinds of crimes of primary interest to proponents of selective incapacitation. Such disengagement from social institutions and relationships was clearly indicated in the present sample by the overall lack of involvement (and stability) in family relations and employment. The reduced social bonds serve to increase the viability of criminal behavior as one of the individual's options by giving him less reason not to take the most expedient and/or direct path to his desired ends in particular situations.

Because of the nature of criminal behavior, however, these reduced social bonds would not be expected to *necessarily* lead to crime. Nor would one expect any resultant criminal behavior patterns to be particularly stable. Again, while in a particular situation, committing a "crime" might appear as the easiest and fastest way of attaining a given end, ordinary "street" crime is unlikely to be seen as a long-term career-line with much potential.[3] Few can expect to get rich snatching purses, robbing gas stations, or burglarizing residences. The risks are high (jail or prison) and the working conditions are generally unsafe and unpleasant. There are few outlets for social recognition associated with mundane criminal behavior. If the career includes violent crimes, there is the likelihood that trusted friends would be scarce. In short, much about crime would seem to make it unattractive as a way of life and little would make someone strive to maintain it as a stable pattern of behavior.

Once an offender is willing to commit crimes in particular situations, it is

---

[3] Drug sales are likely to be an important exception to this simplified characterization.

reasonable that the actual commission of crimes would depend on situational factors, such as the amount of risk involved, the perceived need for a quick solution to a pressing problem, the kinds of other options available, and so on. For these offenders, unskilled (or semi-skilled) and lacking a stable work history, criminal behavior may not even be seen as much worse than the kinds of noncriminal work available. It is not unreasonable that an offender would drift in and out of property crime much like he would drift from one type of low-paying, unpleasant job to another. He may work harder at committing crimes when he needed fast money the most (say, with a developing drug habit) or when working conditions improved (for example, a developing arrangement with a trusted fence or drug supplier). As these situations changed, levels of criminal activity could easily go up or down substantially. Over time, one might expect offense rates to generally decline, peaking now and again at uncharacteristically high levels but returning to lower levels. Eventually, criminal behavior would stop altogether as the opportunities decrease, as less risky means of obtaining goods and services are established, and as incarceration comes to be seen as possibly taking an increasingly larger bite out of the offender's remaining years.

Incarceration, which would be most likely to occur during one of the higher-rate periods, might be expected to have a number of effects. The offender would be incapacitated for some period of time. In addition, the incarceration might be expected to interupt the development of crime-supporting situations and networks, disrupting the patterns of decreasing risk and increasing payoff (or need) that go with them. The offender would return to the streets, literally, a little older and a little wiser, and a little less likely to commit crimes at the rate he was going before being sent to prison. He would not, however, achieve much in the way of increased involvement in the wider social institutions, so that criminal activities would likely remain a viable alternative to noncriminal ones. From this perspective, lower rates of criminal behavior after prison would be expected, but complete rehabilitation would still seem unlikely.

Taking this illustrative exercise one step further, such a perspective would make the general lack of offense-rate predictability that was found for this sample seem more reasonable. The freer the individual is from the normal behavioral restraints associated with social institutions, the more likely his behavior will be determined by more immediate situational influences. In other words, reduced social controls can be expected to lead to unpredictability, at least with respect to the ordinary predictors employed in the present study. On the one hand, one would not expect such situational influences as the isolated involvement in marriages or employment to necessarily inhibit criminal behavior very much; the more pervasive is the disengagement from social institutions, the less that involvement in any *one* of them can be expected to have a profoundly socializing effect. Thus, while these offenders *as a group* were clearly less "bonded" to society than law-abiding citizens, differences among them in this regard may not mean much. More enduring social influences, however, such as those associated with ethnic and cultural differences, would be expected to affect both the nature and relative intensity of criminal behavior. Ethnic differences suggest differences not only in opportunities for legitimate and illegitimate enterprise, but also in ways of dealing with other people. If ethnic groups act differently in other ways, there is little reason to expect that these differences would disappear in the context of committing crimes.

Such a conceptualization of criminal careers is merely illustrative, of course, serving as much to describe as to account for the various trends observed for this sample. One may easily argue about the actual factors that influence the intensity of criminal activity and their relative importance. The main point, however, is that the criminal behavior of the present sample of offenders is best understood from a perspective that emphasizes the importance of situational factors in determining types and rates of criminal behavior. As discussed in the introduction, a "situational" perspective on criminal behavior is inconsistent with current thinking about selective incapacitation. If criminal behavior is situationally determined, different subsamples of offenders would be "high-rate" at different times. Under these conditions, it would be difficult (if not impossible) to identify "high-rate offenders" for differential sentencing. It would also be difficult to take seriously models that forecast the effect of lengthening prison sentences for various offenders, since their behavior cannot be counted on to stay the same.

References

Avi-Itzhak, B., and Shinnar, R. (1973) Quantitative models in crime control. *Journal of Criminal Justice, 1*(3), 185–217.

Blackmore, J., and Welsh, J. (1983) Selective incapacitation: Sentencing according to risk. *Crime and Delinquency*, October, 504–528.

Blumstein, A., and Cohen, J. (1979) Estimation of individual crime rates from arrest records. *The Journal of Criminal Law & Criminology, 70*(4), 561–585.

Blumstein, A., Cohen, J., and Nagin, D. (Eds.) (1978) *Deterrence and incapacitation: Estimating the effects of criminal justice sanctions on crime rates.* Washington, D.C.: National Academy Press.

Blumstein, A., Cohen, J., Roth, J. and Visher, C. (Eds.) (1986) *Criminal careers and "career criminals" (Volume I).* Washington, D.C.: National Academy Press.

Blumstein, A., and Graddy, E. (1982) Prevalence and recidivism in index arrests: A feedback model. *Law and Society Review, 16*, 265–290.

Bursik, R. (1980) The dynamics of specialization in juvenile offenses. *Social Forces, 58*, 851–864.

Chaiken, J., and Chaiken, M. (1982) *Varieties of criminal behavior.* Santa Monica, Ca.: Rand Corporation.

Chaiken, J., and Chaiken, M. (1984) Offender types and public policy. *Crime and Delinquency, 30*(2), 195–224.

Chaiken, J., and Roth, J. (1978) *Selective incapacitation strategies based on estimated crime rates.* Santa Monica, Ca.: Rand Corporation.

Christensen, R. (1967) Projected percentage of U.S. population with criminal arrest and conviction records. In *Task Force Report: Science and Technology*, Report to the President's Commission on Law Enforcement and the Administration of Justice, prepared by the Institute for Defence Analysis. Washington, D.C.: Government Printing Office.

Clear, T., and Barry, D. (1983) Some conceptual issues in incapacitating offenders. *Crime and Delinquency*, October, 529–545.

Cohen, J. (1978) The incapacitative effect of imprisonment: a critical review of the literature. In A. Blumstein, J. Cohen, and D. Nagin (Eds.) *Deterrence and incapacitation: Estimating the effects of criminal justice sanctions on crime rates.* Washington, D.C.: National Academy Press.

Cohen, J. (1983) Incapacitation as a strategy for crime control: Possibilities and pitfalls. In M. Tonry and N. Morris (Eds.), *Crime and justice: An annual review of research, Volume 5.* Chicago: University of Chicago Press.

Cohen, J. (1986) Research on criminal careers: Individual frequency rates and offense seriousness. In A. Blumstein, J. Cohen, J. Roth, and C. Visher (Eds.), *Criminal careers and "career criminals" (Volume I)*. Washington, D.C.: National Academy Press.

Dunford, F., and Elliott, D. (1984) Identifying career offenders using self-reported data. *Journal of Research in Crime and Delinquency, 21* (1), 57–83.

Farrington, D. (1982) Longitudinal analysis of criminal violence. In M. Wolfgang and N. Weiner (Eds.), *Criminal Violence*. Beverly Hills, Ca.: Sage.

Farrington, D. (1983) Offending from 10 to 25 years of age. In K. Van Dusen and S. Mednick (Eds.), *Prospective studies of crime and delinquency*. Boston: Kluwer-Nijhoff.

Farrington, D. (1986) Age and crime. In M. Tonry and N. Morris (Eds.), *Crime and justice: An annual review of research, Volume 7*. Chicago: University of Chicago Press.

Gottfredson, M., and Hirschi, T. (1986) The true value of lambda would appear to be zero: An essay on career criminals, criminal careers, selective incapacitation, cohort studies and related topics. *Criminology, 24* (2), 213–233.

Greenberg, D. (1985) Age, crime and social explanation. *American Journal of Sociology, 91* (1), 1–21.

Greenwood, P., with A. Abrahamse. (1982) *Selective incapacitation*. Santa Monica, Ca.: Rand Corporation.

Haapanen, R., and Jesness, C. (1982) *Early identification of the chronic offender*. Sacramento: California Youth Authority.

Hindelang, M. (1978) Race and involvement in common law personal crimes. *American Sociological Review, 43* (1), 93–109.

Hindelang, M., Hirschi, T., and Weiss, J. (1979) Correlates of delinquency: The illusion of discrepancy between self-report and official measures. *American Sociological Review, 44* (Dec.), 93–109.

Hirschi, T. (1969) *Causes of delinquency*. Berkeley: University of California Press.

Hirschi, T., and Gottfredson, M. (1983) Age and the explanation of crime. *American Journal of Sociology, 89* (3), 552–584.

Hirschi, T., and Gottfredson, M. (1985) Age and crime, logic and scholarship: Comment on Greenberg. *American Journal of Sociology, 91* (1), 22–27.

Janson, C. (1983) Delinquency among metropolitan boys: A progress report. In K. Van Dusen and S. Mednick (Eds.), *Prospective studies in crime and delinquency*. Boston: Kluwer-Nijhoff.

Jesness, C. (1965) *The Fricot Ranch study*. Sacramento: California Youth Authority.

Jesness, C. (1969) *The Preston typology study: Final report*. Sacramento: California Youth Authority.

Jesness, C. (1971a) The Preston typology study: An experiment with differential treatment in an institution. *Journal of Research in Crime and Delinquency, 8*, 38–52.

Jesness, C. (1971b) Comparative effectiveness of two institutional treatment programs for delinquents. *Child Care Quarterly, 1*, 119–130.

Jesness, C. (1975) Comparative effectiveness of behavior modification and transactional analysis programs for delinquents. *Journal of Consulting and Clinical Psychology, 43*, 758–779.

Jesness, C., DeRisi, W. McCormick, P., and Wedge, R. (1972) *The Youth Center research project*. Sacramento: American Justice Institute.

Maltz, M., Gordon, A., McDowell, D., and McCleary, R. (1980) Why before-after comparisons of criminal activity should not be used to evaluate delinquency programs. *Evaluation Review*, April.

Maltz, M., and Pollock S. (1980) Artificial inflation of a poisson rate by a "selection effect." *Operations Research.*

Murray, C., and Cox, L., Jr. (1979) *Beyond probation: Juvenile corrections and the chronic delinquent.* Beverly Hill, Ca.: Sage.

Petersilia, J. (1980) Criminal career research: A review of recent evidence. In M. Tonry and N. Morris (Eds.), *Crime and justice: An annual review of research, Volume 2.* Chicago: University of Chicago Press.

Petersilia, J., and Turner, S., with J. Peterson (1986) *Prison versus probation in California: Implications for crime and offender recidivism.* Santa Monica, Ca.: Rand Corporation.

Peterson, M., and Braiker, H., with S. Polich (1980) *Doing crime: A survey of California prison inmates.* Santa Monica, Ca.: Rand Corporation.

Robins, L. (1966) *Deviant children grown up: A sociological and psychiatric study of sociopathic personality.* Baltimore, Md.: Williams and Wilkins.

Shannon, L. (1982) *Assessing the relationship of adult criminal careers to juvenile careers.* Office of Juvenile Justice and Delinquency Prevention. Washington, D.C.: U.S. Department of Justice.

Shinnar, R., and Shinnar, S. (1975) The effects of the criminal justice system on the control of crime: A quantitative approach. *Law and Society Review, 9* (4), 581–611.

Smith, D., and Smith W. (1984) Patterns of delinquent careers: An assessment of three perspectives, *Social Science Research, 13,* 129–158.

Visher, C. (1986) The Rand inmate survey: A reanalysis. In A. Blumstein, J. Cohen, J. Roth, and C. Visher (Eds.), *Criminal careers and "career criminals" (Volume II).* Washington, D.C.: National Academy Press.

von Hirsch, A., and Gottfredson, D. (1983–84) Selective incapacitation: Some queries about research design and equity. *New York University Review of Law and Social Change, 12* (1), 11–51.

West, D., and Wright, R. (1981) A note on long-term criminal careers. *British Journal of Criminology, 21* (4), 375–376.

Wolfgang, M. (1977) From boy to man—from delinquency to crime. Paper presented at the National Symposium on the Serious Juvenile Offender, Minneapolis, Minnesota. Center for Studies in Criminology and Criminal Law, University of Pennsylvania.

Wolfgang, M., Figlio, R., and Sellin, T. (1972) *Delinquency in a birth cohort.* Chicago: University of Chicago Press.

Wolfgang, M., Thornberry, T., and Figlio, R. (1985) *From boy to man—from delinquency to crime.* Sellin Center for Studies in Criminology and Criminal Law, Wharton School, University of Pennsylvania, Philadelphia.

APPENDIX 1 Sample sizes in pre/post aggregate arrest-rate calculations by race and sample.

Annalysis Type	CYA/ Prob	CYA/ CDC	Suppl/ Prob	Suppl/ CDC	Total Sample
Pre/post rates					
Pre-period					
No data		(5)			
White	88	219	39	76	422
Black	30	180	35	70	315
Hispanic	22	82	22	28	154
Other	(2)	(6)	(2)	(1)	
Total (Race anal.)	140	481	96	174	891
Post-period					
No data	(6)	(43)	(1)		
White	84	206	39	76	405
Black	28	162	35	70	295
Hispanic	22	75	21	28	146
Other	(2)	(6)	(2)	(1)	
Total (Race anal.)	134	443	95	174	847
Yearly rates					
Pre-period					
1st year	133	485	91	174	883
2nd year	133	464	87	168	852
3rd year	123	408	83	148	762
4th year	115	342	74	114	645
4-year rates	133	485	91	174	883
Post-period					
1st year post	136	449	97	175	857
2nd year post	131	431	96	175	833
3rd year post	117	404	96	175	792
4th year post	105	369	94	174	742
4-year rates	136	449	97	175	857

APPENDIX 2 Means, standard deviations, and number of cases included in age-block variables: All cases with prison or probation information.

	N	Mean	Standard deviation
% Street Time			
18–21	907	63.83	26.65
22–25	907	55.93	33.43
26–29	856	69.31	33.47
30–33	588	80.43	29.00
34–37	393	85.24	31.56
% Time: Heroin Use			
18–21	835	28.51	40.97
22–25	697	31.75	44.10
26–29	670	21.21	37.68
30–33	499	7.28	22.93
34–37	283	2.32	13.49
% Time: Uppers/Downers Use			
18–21	835	31.46	42.12
22–25	697	26.70	41.60
26–29	670	16.71	34.43
30–33	499	5.59	20.41
34–37	283	1.11	9.25
% Time: Hallucinogens Use			
18–21	835	57.93	44.96
22–25	697	53.57	46.57
26–29	670	33.74	42.61
30–33	499	9.94	26.31
34–37	283	2.89	15.77
% Time: Common-law			
18–21	907	14.77	29.50
22–25	907	17.62	31.76
26–29	893	14.19	28.54
30–33	805	5.27	17.70
34–37	553	.81	5.49
% Time: Legally Married			
18–21	907	14.10	28.00
22–25	907	18.62	32.71
26–29	893	14.27	29.19
30–33	805	5.72	18.92
34–37	553	.89	5.95
% Time: Supporting Dependents			
18–21	907	15.81	29.68
22–25	907	21.60	35.50
26–29	893	16.48	31.91
30–33	805	6.30	20.41
34–37	553	1.07	7.08

	N	Mean	Standard deviation
% Time: Employed Full-time			
18–21	835	12.94	23.91
22–25	697	17.16	28.10
26–29	670	11.68	23.75
30–33	499	3.86	14.34
34–37	283	.60	4.92
% Time: Unemployed			
18–21	835	74.65	32.32
22–25	697	72.55	32.81
26–29	670	81.46	29.35
30–33	499	93.58	18.60
34–37	283	99.19	54.98
Background Information			
Criminality:			
Father	907	.14	.35
Siblings	907	.43	.50
Age at first:			
Arrest	846	13.89	3.63
Commitment	875	16.01	3.57
No. escapes	762	.77	1.22
Claimed school			
grade	862	10.55	1.74
Adult prison	907	.74	.44

APPENDIX 3 Means, standard deviations, and number of cases included in pre/post variables: All cases with prison or probation information.

	N	Mean	Standard deviation
Arrest Rate (Post)			
Total	821	1.02	.70
Violent	821	.31	.43
Violent-economic	821	.17	.33
Property	821	.36	.49
Arrest Rate (Pre)			
Total	862	1.49	.65
Violent	862	.46	.49
Violent-economic	862	.26	.39
Property	862	.59	.53
% Time (Pre)			
Heroin use	882	27.04	41.10
Upper/downers use	882	26.89	40.62
Hallucinogens use	882	54.58	46.15
Common-law relationship	882	16.38	30.91
Legally married	882	18.41	33.26
Employed	892	23.13	30.85
Not incarcerated (street time)	886	76.00	23.93
% Time (Post)			
Heroin use	870	23.24	40.80
Upper/downers use	870	19.84	38.45
Hallucinogens use	870	38.91	47.17
Common-law relationship	870	13.70	29.97
Legally married	870	15.10	30.55
Employed	708	24.90	29.89
Background Information			
Number of siblings	852	4.47	2.78
Known welfare recipient	907	.17	.38
Intact family	907	.43	.50
Any criminality (father)	907	.14	.35
Any criminality (mother)	907	.04	.21
Any criminality (siblings)	907	.43	.50
Age at first arrest	846	13.89	3.63
Age at first commitment	875	16.01	3.57
Number of prior escapes	762	.77	1.23
Number of drugs (juvenile)	907	1.48	1.74
Any juvenile drug use	907	.57	.50
Race (Coded 0,1)			
White	907	.47	.50
Hispanic	907	.35	.48
Black	907	.17	.38
Commitment Offense			
Includes Robbery (0,1)	907	.29	.45
Includes Burglary (0,1)	907	.33	.47
Number of crimes	907	1.55	2.31

	N	Mean	Standard deviation
Prior Conviction			
For Robbery (0,1)	907	.08	.28
For Burglary (0,1)	907	.26	.44
Rand Score			
Robbers	260	4.12	1.33
Burglars	295	4.18	1.75
Current Term (CDC Cases Only n = 667)			
Age at entry	667	21.95	2.60
Age at release	667	24.91	2.96
Length of stay (mos.)	667	35.51	27.60
Juv. comm. (CYA) (0,1)	667	.74	.44
No. of disciplinaries	602	6.52	9.40
Serious disciplinary	667	.24	.43
Known enemies (0,1)	667	.17	.38
Known gang affiliation (0,1)	667	.09	.29

Index

Research in Criminology

continued

Multiple Problem Youth:
Delinquency, Substance Use, and Mental Health Problems
D.S. Elliott, D. Huizinga and S. Menard

Selective Incapacitation and the Serious Offender:
A Longitudinal Study of Criminal Career Patterns
Rudy A. Haapanen